Georges Poisson

General Inspector des Musées de la Ville de Paris

PARIS during the REVOLUTION

1789 - 1989

Also by Georges Poisson

Les musées de France, Paris, Presses universitaires, coll. Que sais-je? 3ᵉ éd. 1976.
Evocation du Grand Paris, 3t., Paris, Ed. de minuit, 1955-61.
Histoire et histoires de Sceaux, préf. de Georges Duhamel, Sceaux, 3ᵉ éd., 1981.
Châteaux de la Loire, Paris, 3ᵉ éd. 1972.
Châteaux d'Ile-de-France, Paris, Balland, 1968. Ed. allemande: Munich, 1968.
Le Val de Marne, Paris, Ed. de minuit, 1958. Couronné par l'Académie française.
Album Saint-Simon, Paris, Bibl. de la Pléiade, 1969.
Monsieur de Saint-Simon, Paris, Fayard, 3ᵉ éd., 1987.
Histoire des grands boulevards, Paris, Le Cadratin, 1980. Couronné par l'Académie française.
Guide des maisons d'hommes célèbres, Paris, Pierre Horay, 3ᵉ éd., 1988.
Dix siècles à Montfort-l'Amaury (avec M.H. Hadrot), préf. de Jacques de Lacretelle, Montfort-l'Amaury, 1983. Couronné par l'Académie française.
Choderlos de Laclos ou l'obstination, Paris, Grasset, 2ᵉ éd., 1986. Bourse Goncourt de la Biographie 1985.
Cette curieuse famille d'Orléans, Paris, Perrin, 2ᵉ éd., 1977.
L'Elysée, histoire d'un palais, Paris, Perrin, 2ᵉ éd., 1988. Couronné par l'Académie française.
Monte-Cristo, un château de roman, préf. d'Alain Decaux, Marly-le-roi, éd. Champflour, 1987.

© Copyright 1989 by
CASA EDITRICE BONECHI
Via Cairoli, 18/b - 50131 Firenze - Italy
Telex 571323 CEB

No part of this work may be reproduced or utilized without the prior written permission of the publisher.

All rights reserved.

Editor, photographic research and bibliographical résumés:
Hubert Brissonneau.

Typesetting:
"m & m" Fotocomposizione - Florence

Photolithography:
Studio Del Panta - Florence

Translation:
Erika Pauli for Studio Comunicare, Florence

Printed in the EEC
by the Centro Stampa Editoriale Bonechi

Diffusion:
OVET PARIS
13, Rue des Nanettes Paris 11ᵉ
Tél. 43.385.680

Dépôt légal IIIᵉ trimestre 1989

INTRODUCTION

The French Revolution was unquestionably the one period in history which aroused as much enthusiasm as it did censure. Passions and opinions ran high, either celebrating or condemning it *en bloc*. Eventually an attempt at impartiality suggested the idea of an initial good revolution followed by a bad revolution, with a dividing line that varied, depending on the individual, from the date of the first crime to that of the homicidal despotism.

Today, the still vivid recollections of the revolutionary episodes so many of us have lived through in the last half century, both in France and elsewhere, help us to realize that, on the one hand, it is often the minorities who forcibly impose new concepts, and, on the other, that excess is practically inseparable from political change, for, at one and the same time, honest partisans become drunk on violence, and disorders automatically attract the dregs of society.

This relativity of events throughout the centuries and on all continents counsels the historian to remain a neutral observer: his task is that of narrating, understanding, explaining. Let us try to do likewise, essentially for Paris, since this was where the Revolution as a whole took place.

This guide is just as much about the monuments that once were, and the places where they stood, as it is about those other visible signs of the Revolution which still haunt the streets of Paris. The description of each individual monument and site and of the events that took place there is accompanied by illustrations taken from old documents, paintings or prints, as well as by contemporary views which help us to identify what still exists as we wander through the city.

A historical introduction whose purpose is to recall the essential events of the Revolution in their chronological order is followed by a presentation of the places and monuments which witnessed them. To facilitate the visit, these have been classified and numbered in line with a continuous itinerary that is punctuated by the salient sites, such as the Bastille, Place de Grève, the Tuileries. Place de la Révolution, Champ de Mars, and the Conciergerie. To simplify the reading, these places have been grouped into districts, and each number set at the beginning of a text refers to the map at the end of the book, helping the visitor to know exactly where each monument is to be found.

Lastly, a dictionary of the personages cited in the text furnishes a general synopsis of the life of each one and the part they played in the politics and history of the Revolution.

▷ **Opening of the Estates-general on May 5, 1789 in Versailles** (engraving by Helman, Bibliothèque des Arts décoratifs).

THE REVOLUTION IN THE HISTORY OF PARIS

THE FALL OF THE BASTILLE

July 1789

Louis XVI, the ancien régime — *The French monarchic system had run out of resources. It had not been capable either of reforming itself or of ensuring an operative continuity in line with its doctrines and had ended up by displaying nothing but one shortcoming after the other: financial inadequacy, administrative inadequacy, a lack of ideas, a lack of competence, of responsibility, of authority. A regime that could be likened to a worm-eaten statue, ready to crumble at the slightest touch, and whose symbol, despite futile attempts at rehabilitation, was the sorrowful figure of Louis XVI. This prince, full of good intentions, but unable to see them through or to impose a policy, was, from the convocation of the Parlement in 1774 to the Swiss massacre on August 10th, the man of one abdication after the other. As they gradually tired of these inconsistencies, which at times seemed to amount to treason, the French finally abandoned the last of the forty kings who had made France what it was to a fate he obviously did not merit.*

The summoning of the estates-general — *As in all the balloting that took place up to 18 Brumaire, there were more abstentions than votes when the estates-general were elected. Throughout its history, the Revolution was to be the doing of one minority after the other, each, in turn, unfailingly torn to pieces. Poorly prepared, badly organized, these estates could however have opened the way to salvation if the king had only been capable of fostering the formation of a moderate majority in the Assembly with himself at its head. But beginning with the "Tennis Court oath" (Jeu de Paume, June 20), the royal court took up its stand on one side, the progressive deputies on the other, and the abyss between them was never bridged.*

The fall of the Bastille — *The clumsy dismissal of Necker*

3

◁ **Sack of the Invalides** (J. B. Lallemand, Musée Carnavalet). The morning of July 14th the insurgents invade the Hôtel des Invalides in search of arms.

▵ **Liberation of the Prisoners from the Bastille** (engraving, Musée Carnavalet). This episode took place in Rue Saint-Antoine, at the exit of the fortress. On the right, the Convent of the Visitation.

▷ **The Taking of the Bastille** (French school, late 18th cent., Musée de Versailles). In the foreground, the arrest of de Launay, governor of the fortress, who was later massacred.

by the authorities on July 12th set off an immediate reaction in Paris: at the Royal Palace, the center of all the turmoil and all the vices, Camille Desmoulins incited the crowd. The royal power immediately backed down, but the revolt was already under way. Two days afterwards the Bastille was taken. Now, two centuries later, we are still struck more by the symbolic force of that action than by the blood spilled or by the futility of the results. Three days later, the visit of the monarch to Paris ratified this coup de force *and thereafter the uncontrollable elements typical of all revolutions sporadically began to appear. On the 23rd of July, Foulon and Bertier were massacred with refined cruelty, while the parallel power of the clubs and the sections gradually took hold.*

△ **The King on his Way to the Hôtel de Ville on July 17, 1789** (Prieur, drawing, Musée Carnavalet).

◁ **Louis XVI at the Balcony of the Palace of Versailles Promising to Return to Paris, on October 6, 1789** (engraving, Cabinet des Estampes).

The days of October — *These last two (the movement seems to have begun in the district of the Cordeliers) were responsible for the tragic piece of buffoonery that was staged on October 5th. A procession, led by market women, set out for Versailles to bring the king back to Paris. The Assembly, in the wake of the returning sovereign, set up its headquarters in the hall of the archbishop's residence, then in the Manège (Riding School) of the Tuileries, where it continued its work of gigantic reform. On November 2nd, the possessions of the clergy were nationalized, and the assignats were issued, as a corollary. On December 22nd, the* départements *were created. Two months earlier, one of the first clubs, created in Versailles, had moved to a convent in Paris, from which it took its name, or rather nickname, of Jacobins. On the left bank, another club, the Cordeliers, had come into being a few months thereafter, with Danton and Marat, and was immediately distinguished by its more revolutionary and disorderly point of view.*

THE CONSTITUENT ASSEMBLY
(July 1789 - September 1791)

The Fête de la Fédération — *Summer of 1790 marks a turning point, a pause accompanied by a precarious agreement. On July 14th, at the Champ de Mars, the Fête de la Fédération, presided over by the king, had as its scope the reconciliation of all the citizens, marked by an enthusiasm even the rain did not succeed in dampening. Yet the Civil Constitution of the Clergy, the direct cause of the fracture, had been voted that very eve, the mass was celebrated by Talleyrand, a psychologically warped bishop, and a group of sturdy young men, armed with knives, hoisted banners reading "Tremble, aristocrats, here are the young butchers!".*
Despite all this the king serenely passed the summer at Saint-Cloud and the Assembly continued its work: the Parlamentarians, who had so strongly backed the Revolution, decided to stay there.

The flight to Varennes — *This is the great period of the Jacobins, a veritable parallel power of whose danger neither the king nor the Assembly were fully aware. Intoxicated by their success and importance, the deputies were much more concerned with turning the future constitution into a weapon against the absolutism of the king, which was to all effects already obsolete, than with making it a defense against the popular despotism that was gradually coming to a head. The Jacobins made them vote as they pleased, while the rabble was under the control of the popular societies. When, in April 1791, the royal family decided to return to Saint-Cloud, an insurrection prevented them from doing so and neither the king nor the* municipalité *were able to impose their will. It was then that Louis XVI, tormented by scruples of conscience, began to think of flight: on June 21st, a poorly organized and badly led expedition took the royal family as far as Varennes, where it was immediately arrested. The French monarchy, opprobriously brought back to Paris, was in its death throes. Time and again in the history of the Capetians the king knew no better way of overcoming the wrath of the Parisians than to leave his capital. M. Thiers was to take note of this lesson.*
For some, however, this pitiful attempt which had definitely ruined Louis XVI's personal prestige, strangely enough reinforced the symbol of what he stood for. Varennes marked the split between the first Republicans and the moderate deputies, who at this point considered the king a defense. The bourgeoisie of the Assembly, who, thanks to the constitution they had created, had supplanted the aristocracy in the state of the realm, saw victory within their grasp and thought only of exploiting the Revolution to their own advantage. A perjured and discredited king could serve as alibi and shield against a

▽ **The Fête de la Fédération on July 14, 1790 in the Champ de Mars** (engraving by Helman, Musée Carnavalet). In the center, the altar on which Talleyrand celebrated mass. On the far right, the royal tribune.

△ **The Royal Family Returns from Varennes on June 25, 1789** (engraving, Bibliothèque des Arts décoratifs). On the left, the monument to Louis XV by Bouchardon and Pigalle, which was destroyed the following year.

◁ **Proclamation of the Constitution, Place des Innocents, September 18, 1791** (Prieur, drawing, Musée Carnavalet). The famous fountain of the Innocents, rebuilt on a square ground plan a few years earlier, can be seen in the background.

Republic that could be fatal to holders of property. On July 16, Barnave prevailed: the king was exculpated.
The insurrection of Champ de Mars — *Initially the realist bourgeoisie had the upper hand and the republican insurrection was put down in blood in the Champ de Mars on July 17th. That evening, one of their leaders, Maximilian Robespierre, took lodging at the home of the cabinet-maker Duplay at 398 Rue Saint-Honoré, while the moderate elements of the Jacobins split off and set themselves up in the old convent of the Feuillants.*
The constitution of year I — *This neo-monarchic fervor continued for several weeks. The Assembly finished drawing up the constitution, and restored limited powers to the king. After having ratified the text, which was accepted by Louis XVI on September 14, 1791, it was dissolved and ceded its place on October 1st to the first assembly of the new regime, the Legislative. The Revolution seemed to have achieved its scope with the installation of the constitutional monarchy. It lasted only ten months.*

THE LEGISLATIVE ASSEMBLY

(October 1791 - September 1792)

While the work of the Legislative Assembly during this period was often quite useful, it also shouldered the terrible responsibility, on April 20, 1792, together with the king and the new Girondin ministers, of committing the country to war. From now on the unfolding of events in Paris was conditioned by the ministry, which was to survive the Revolution, and was in part responsible for the Terror.

The invasion of the Tuileries — *The revolutionary forces had not however laid down their arms, and methodically assaulted the sections and the National Guard. The new mayor of Paris, Pétion, was secretly trying to subvert the legal power by means of riots. On June 20th, the Tuileries were invaded, as a reaction to the king's refusal to approve various decrees, and Louis XVI was obliged to wear the cap of liberty* (bonnet rouge) *and to drink a toast with the rebels. Like all his ancestors, however, he was courageous and refused to retract, holding firm in the face of the vociferous crowd for several hours and forcing it to withdraw.*

The Nation in danger — *It was clear that the insurrection still lacked the strength to overthrow the established power. The National Guard, on the whole, remained constitutional, and a certain amount of reaction and indignation was manifested in favor of the king. But at the same time, the war was coming closer, the frontiers were threatened and on July 11th the Assembly declared that the nation was in danger and did all it could to galvanize the country's forces. On Sunday the 22nd, the cannons thundering hourly from the Pont Neuf and the Arsenal, the call-to-arms was sounded in all the quarters. At the crossings, city officials surrounded by banners and music, read proclamations. In the squares, boards set on drums in the midst of a semicircle of flags were used to receive enlistments. In three days more than three thousand men were recruited in Paris.*

The insurrectional Commune and the taking of the Tuileries — *In the grips of the foreign threat, suspicious — and rightly so — that the king would come to terms with the enemy, exasperated by the arrogance of the émigrés, which in the end was why the royal family and*

▽ **Invasion of the Tuileries on June 20, 1792** (engraving by Berthault, Musée Carnavalet).

the royalists were considered "internal enemies", the Republicans thought that the salvation of France depended on a clean sweep of the regime. The Girondins, long faithful to the king, but who expected a military victory to solve all the current difficulties (particularly economic) and who thought it would enable them to take over the power once and for all, realized that if need be Louis XVI must be sacrificed, and that they had to appeal to the people, without whose participation success in the field of battle was impossible.

The leaders of this new Revolution, with Danton at their head, realized that the coup de force *had to be scrupulously prepared, and sought outside aid. The deputy Barbaroux asked the mayor of Marseilles for six hundred men who were ready to die.*

They arrived on July 30th, singing the famous hymn by Rouget de Lisle, the Marseillaise. *The military action was methodically organized, just to be sure, in two stages.*

The constitutional party, on its part, knew there would be an attack and bided its time. The new commander of the

◁ **Day of June 20, 1792 at the Tuileries** (engraving, Cabinet des Estampes).

◁ **Recruiting on the Pont-neuf, July 18, 1792** (engraving by Berthault, Musée Carnavalet).

▽ **The Taking of the Tuileries, August 10, 1792** (engraving by Berthault, Musée Carnavalet). The assault on the Palace as seen by an eye-witness.

National Guard, the loyalist Mandat, had called to the Tuileries nine hundred Swiss, several hundred body guards, and national guards for a total of one thousand five hundred true and tried men who were stationed around the palace.

The night of August 9-10th, while Pétion was playing one side off against the other, the bells from the south and east called the sections to the insurrection, and twenty-eight of them sent their delegates to the Hôtel de Ville to take their positions near the regular municipalité *and replace them. Thus was born the illegal revolutionary Commune which was to last until 9 Thermidor. Convoked to the town hall, Mandat was removed from office, arrested, immediately massacred. He was the only man capable of defending the regime and the king.*

At the Tuileries fighting began the morning of August 10th. The famous Marseillais were unable to break through the Swiss Guard which firmly held the palace. But the king, confused or irresponsible, in any case once more superceded, decided after an hour to flee with his family, taking nothing with him, and to seek refuge with the Assembly. He was seen crossing the garden, and the unknown Captain Bonaparte murmered: — Che coglione... (What an ass...).

The royal family huddled together in the quarters of the Assembly secretaries, where it sweltered day after day. In the meanwhile the Swiss, despite the arrival of Santerre's troops, who had come from the Faubourg Saint-Antoine, continued to resist as long as their munitions held out. Upon request of the Assembly, the king, whose last decision this was, had a note sent ordering them to cease fire. He might just as well have asked them to blow their

brains out: the moment they stopped firing they were massacred.

For two days, the palace of the Tuileries was plundered, devastated, degraded, sullied, humiliated, inundated with the blood of all its inhabitants, whether they were lackeys, servants, or stable boys. During this period the royal family continued to pass its days in the back rooms of the Assembly, its nights in the convent of the Feuillants. On the 13th, the Legislative Assembly decided to hand the king and his family over to their worst enemy, the Commune of Paris, which shut them up in the tower of the Temple. And on the 21st the guillotine began its work, while one after the other, news of the invasion of the north, of the fall of Longwy, and of the first Vendean insurrection reached Paris.

Finally aware of what was happening, on August 29th, the Assembly decided to dismiss the insurrectional Commune. But entrenched in its power and its armed forces, the latter refused to break up and replied with the massacres of September.

The massacres in the prisons — *Between the 2nd and the 5th of that month, one thousand two hundred persons were killed in the Paris prisons, old or improvised: the Abbaye, the Carmes, the Salpêtrière, la Force, and beyond the barriers, Bicêtre, with children "who seemed never to die". At the Carmes, about a hundred priests; at la Force, the Princess de Lamballe, decapitated on a milestone and whose head, stuck on a pike, was presented to the royal family through a window in the Temple. Yet most of those condemned had been detained for common crimes, which makes what happened even harder to understand. Who was responsible? Marat, who boasted of the action? Fabre d'Eglantine, who approved? Danton, the strong man of the new government, who kept his hands off? More than anything it was a hysteria of blood and hate which had grown throughout the twenty-two months until it reached the breaking point.*

▽ **Destruction of the Statue of Louis XIV, Place des Victoires** (Prieur, drawing, Musée Carnavalet). On August 12, 1792 the statues of Henry IV, on the Pont-neuf, of Louis XIII, Place Royale, of Louis XIV, Place des Victoires and Place Vendôme, were toppled and destroyed by the insurgents.

In the grip of this Terror, Paris abstained from the elections of the new assembly, called, in imitation of the Americans, Convention. Marat's entire list won, with Robespierre, Danton, Collot d'Herbois, Billaud-Varennes and, lastly, the duke of Orléans, now known as Philippe Egalité who had, like his cousin, been discredited.

△ **The Grand Châtelet** (Naudet, water-color, Musée Carnavalet). The fortress of the Grand Châtelet, on the site of the square with the same name, was long used as a prison. It was one of the stages on which the massacres of September 1792 were acted out.

THE CONVENTION
(September 1792 - October 1795)

Gironde and Montagne — *On September 20, 1792, the Convention met in the Manège where in its first session it proclaimed the abolition of the Monarchy, but affirmed respect for property, the* leitmotif *of the entire Revolution, and which Robespierre himself tried in vain to have emended. Brissot and his friends formed the right wing of the Assembly, continued to declare themselves revolutionaries, but above all enemies of the Commune, which had installed its men on the left, on the benches of the Montagne (or Mountain). Between the two, a center, a swamp (Marais or Plaine) of trembling opportunists. The struggle between the two, who immediately came to blows, also took on a geographic character: the Girondins, adversaries of the Commune, liberal and legalist, clearly hoping to suspend the course of the Revolution, sought the backing of the provincial administrations, denying the supremacy of Paris, while the Montagnards, closer to the people, took advantage, in the face of danger, of denouncing this dispersion of forces, this attack on a unity that was more than ever necessary, and put forward a claim to the concentration of power in the hands of a few Parisian representatives. The Montagne, offshoot of the Commune, was to lay hold of the dictatorship with a hand of iron.*

The execution of the King — *The Convention immediately succeeded in having charges brought against the king. Unkempt (his razors had been taken away from him), Louis was unable to reply to the accusations, only too well founded, of perjury and treason, and was trapped in negations that were sometimes obviously false (he declared he did not recognize the key to the iron chest which had a label written in his own hand). The outcome of a death penalty without reprieve was obtained by a majority of one vote cast by Philippe Egalité. One of the regicide deputies, Le Peletier de St-Fargeau, was assassinated in the royal palace the day after. On January 21, 1793, a green coach under strong escort led the prisoner through the boulevards, as far as Place Louis XV, now called Place de la Révolution, where the guillotine had been raised.*

The triumph of Marat — *The revolutionaries had burned their bridges and had no choice but headlong flight, so to say, ahead, impelling and intransigent, for the enemy was once more at the frontiers. On February 24, 1793 the Convention decreed a conscription of 300,000 men and, on April 6th, the Comité de Salut public (Committee of Public Safety) was created, which took up headquarters*

▷ **Triumph of Marat** (Louis-Léopold Boilly, painting, Musée des Beaux-arts, Lille). On leaving the Revolutionary Tribunal after being acquitted, the tribune is carried in triumph in the Grand'Salle of the Palais de Justice (April 24, 1793).

▽ **The Execution of Louis XVI** (engraving by Helman, Musée Carnavalet). On the right, the base where the statue of Louis XV formerly stood.

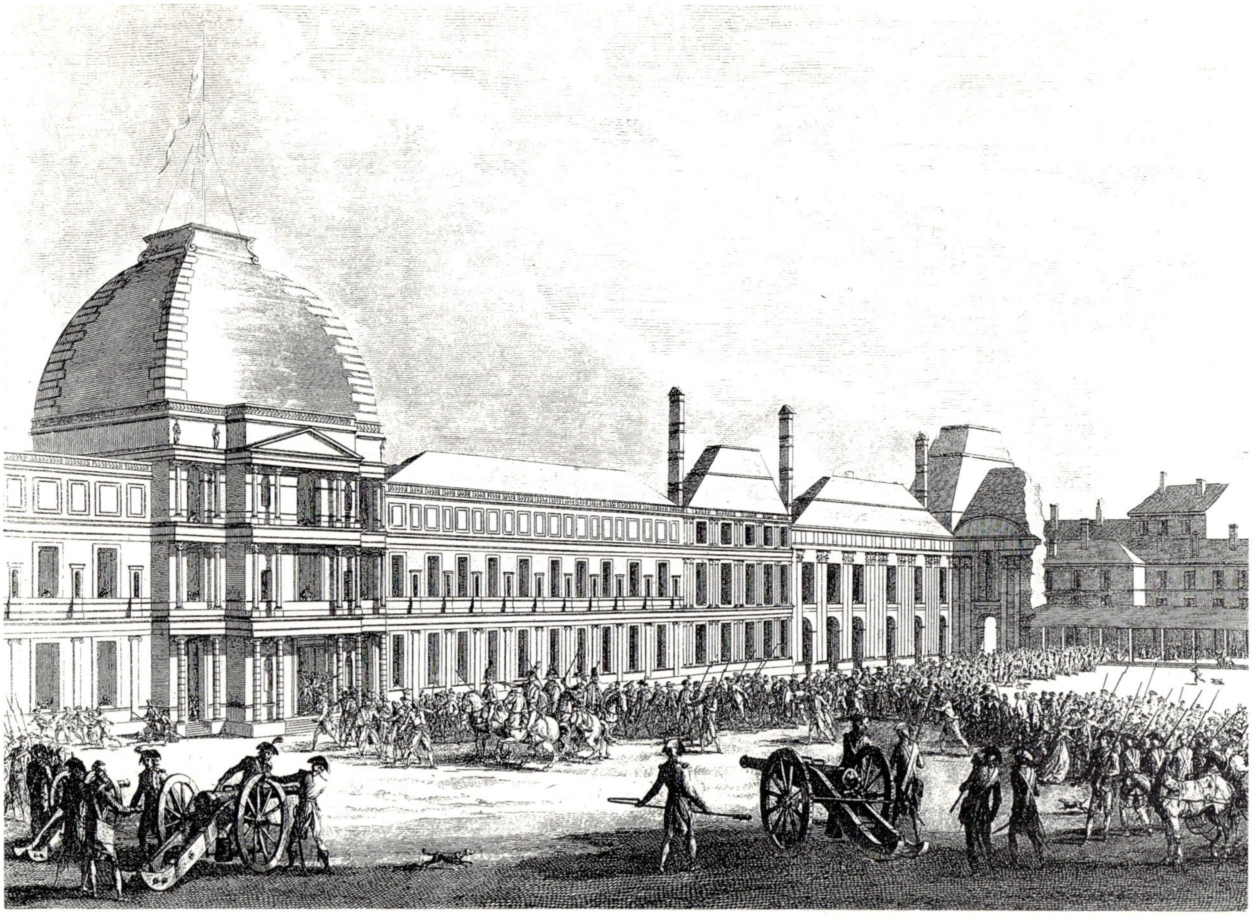

△ **Arrest of the Girondins on June 2, 1793** (engraving by Berthault, Musée Carnavalet). The troops of the Commune, under the command of Hanriot, besiege the Tuileries where the Convention is in session.

▷ **An execution in the Place de la Révolution in 1793-94** (P. A. Demachy, Musée Carnavalet, detail).

in the Pavillon de Flore. At the same time, the Montagnards conducted a violent campaign against the Girondins, who still held the majority. On April 14th they retaliated by bringing Marat before the Revolutionary Court, created the month before, but the Commune, drumming up all its forces, succeeded in winning acquittal, and the victor, back at the Convention, asked for the heads of the Girondins, whose imprudence had caused their downfall.

The arrest of the Girondin deputies — On June 2nd, Marat launched the army of the revolutionary sections against the Assembly. In command was Hanriot, an old servant who had been promoted general the day before. The troops assaulted the old hall of the Machines in the Tuileries, where the Convention had been installed on May 9th, and when the deputies attempted to leave, preceded by their president Hérault de Séchelles, about to pronounce a harangue, Hanriot beat him to the draw:
— The people did not rise up to listen to fine phrases! And, "with a shout loud enough to subdue an entire square", commanded:
— Gunners, at your posts!

△ **Promenade of Prisoners in Sainte-Pélagie in 1794** (Hubert Robert, Musée Carnavalet). Sainte-Pélagie, on the site of the present Mosque, was one of the numerous Revolutionary prisons. Hubert Robert was interned here during the Terror.

The Convention was forced to reopen session and turn over the Girondins. Twenty-one went to the block, others were hunted down and died miserably. A fate, shared shortly thereafter, by their muse, Mme Roland.
Marat did not live long to enjoy his victory. On July 13th, a young Norman girl, Charlotte Corday, who had bought a sturdy carving knife at the Palais Royal, gained access to the tribune's house, opposite the Cordeliers, and killed him. David organized a funeral of barbaric splendor.
The Committee of Public Safety had been reshuffled and now included Couthon, Saint-Just, Lindet, Prieur de la Côte d'or, Carnot, Barère, Collot d'Herbois, Billaud-Varennes and, after July 24th, Robespierre. They were flanked, in a neighboring house, by another committee, that of the Sûreté Générale (General Security) which, being more mysterious, may have been even more powerful.
The Terror — *The action of the committee during its year-long term might perhaps be summed up in two words: fear and energy - fear of the enemies at home and abroad, suspected allies of the former, fear of the opposition, of conspiracies, of anything that might, even in the least, hamper the action of power, a fear quite often imaginary. The one remedy capable of coping with this situation was the Terror, whose scope was that of eliminating the declared enemies or of discouraging potential enemies, the famous* suspects *(law of September 17). France had to lie under the cloak of terror in order to give free rein to a government which was well aware of the fact that it was a contested minority government, faced with enormous problems, both within and without, and that whatever it accomplished seemed a miracle. History teaches us that a minority government always has to defend itself: the one of year II illustrates the axiom to perfection.*
This period is characterized by two aspects which have been variously stressed, depending on the historian. On one hand, action, unquestionably disorderly, but terribly impelling and efficacious, in the service of a France at war both at home and abroad, with an administration that was once more reshuffled and centralized, constantly battling the rising prices with the law on the Maximum, mass conscription including the institution of obligatory military service, the formation of improvised armies that were controlled by agents on mission and galvanized by threat and example (various generals were beheaded for incompetence not at all manifest).
The national defense — *There was a shortage of everything needed to equip the voluntaries and Paris became the arsenal of France. Two hundred fifty-eight smithies*

△ **Execution of Marie Antoinette on October 16, 1793**
(engraving by Helman, Bibliothèque des Arts décoratifs).

were set up outside, at Luxembourg, the Tuileries, in Place de la Révolution. While the women seated at the threshold of their houses, in that summer of 1793, sewed gaiters, cut sacks and tents, the men blew on the forges and hammered the iron. More than five thousand men were employed in these improvised workshops which produced 146,630 guns and pistols between November of 1793 and December of 1794. Since the necessary gunpowder was also lacking, on August 28th the Committee for Public Safety launched a vast campaign for the collection of saltpetre throughout France, and, appealing to all the inventors willing to aid the national defense, experimented their inventions in the château de Meudon, under the direction of a general-writer, Choderlos de Laclos.

The despotism of Robespierre — The other aspect is the one best known: an abject policy of the decimation of the élite, the overcrowded Paris prisons, mockery of justice, and the guillotine functioning at an increasing pace from day to day. Those who went to the scaffold, one after the other, included Marie Antoinette, Philippe Egalité, Mme Elisabeth, Mme du Barry, Lavoisier, Malesherbes, Hébert, Chaumette and their friends, Bailly, Hérault de Sechelles, Danton, Camille Desmoulins and his wife Lucile, Barnave, André Chénier.

The greatest mistake of the Committee of Public Safety may have been that of having prolonged and accentuated a Terror which was no longer justifiable, for the situation both abroad and in the Vendée was returning to normality. Undoubtedly Robespierre thought it was still necessary, both for his attempt to strengthen the centralization as well as for the application of the social policy outlined in the laws of Ventôse: both social and political, for the Incorruptible (as Robespierre was called) thereby hoped to distribute the confiscated property of the enemies of the regime among the poor and with this great transferral of property turn the passive (non-voting) citizens into active (voting) citizens, and thus provide a majority basis for his regime. But the realm of Virtue could be established only in blood and from 22 Ventôse (March 12) on there were daily meetings between Robespierre and the public prosecutor Fouquier-Tinville, who was after his ration of heads.

△ **Robespierre in the Antechamber of the Committee of Public Safety** (engraving, Musée Carnavalet). Transferred during the night to the Tuileries where he was left unattended for several hours, Robespierre went to the guillotine the next day.

Nor did the Incorruptible give in to clemency. The Dantonians, who recommended the end of the Terror, went to the scaffold on April 5th. Even so, Robespierre, with the application of his decrees, attempted to restore a semblance of reason to the policies of the revolutionary tribunal, but he was barely heeded, a dictator whose power lay more in words than in facts. The precarious nature of his position became clearly evident on the day of the Fête of the Supreme Being, June 8, 1794, when as president of the Convention, in other words head of state, he adhered to the style of the manifestations of the time. But in point of fact he was materially isolated, separated from his associates, which may even have been what they wanted.

The Terror continued at an ever-increasing rate: 15 death sentences in Vendémiaire, 65 in Brumaire, 116 in Ventôse, 155 in Germinal, 354 in Floréal. On 22 Prairial (June 10) a law suppressed the last guarancies of justice that had remained for those accused and left nothing but one unequivocable sentence: death. And five days later, to spare the Parisians who lived in the center of the city and had had all they could stand of seeing the tumbril go by day after day, the guillotine was transferred to the Place du Trône renversé, and the corpses were buried in the gardens of Picpus. Halucinated, increasingly isolated, even within the circle of his complices, obsessed by the idea of an absolute, almost divine, power, he was haunted by the idea that all that stood in his way were men and women who had to be eliminated, but who seemed to spring back as fast as they were repressed.

The fall of Robespierre — *A period of uncertainty followed and from 15 Messidor (July 7) on Robespierre, aware that his influence was on the wane, began to desert the sessions of the Committee. His attempt to once more take over the reins was fatal. On 8 Thermidor (July 26) he pronounced a discourse in great style at the Convention but made the mistake of threatening without naming names: everyone felt threatened. That night, Fréron, Tallien, Barras came to an agreement with the eternal timid sheep of the Marais and when Robespierre once more appeared at the Assembly the next day, he was met by a majority determined to kill in order not to be killed. He*

△ **Insurrection of I Prairial** (engraving by Berthault, Musée Carnavalet). The insurrectionists invade the hall of the Convention at the Tuileries and massacre the deputy Féraud.

◁ **Mobs at the Faubourg Saint-Antoine on 4 Prairial year III** (engraving by Berthault, Cabinet des Estampes).

▷ **Defense of the Convention on 13 Vendémiaire** (Lebarbier, drawing, Musée Carnavalet). The troops of Barras prepare to hold out against the Royalist rebels. In the back, the gallery overlooking the Seine. On the right, the palace of the Tuileries.

was not allowed to speak, he was insulted, a ferocious war cry was raised against him. Arrested together with Saint-Just, Couthon, Le Bas, he was taken away by the gendarmes of the Convention at half past five in the afternoon.

At seven, they were free, and masters of Paris, had they wanted. At Luxembourg the prison guards refused to receive them and the Commune, ringing the tocsin, called together its troops. Led to the City Hall, Robespierre was asked to sign a call to arms.

— In whose name? asked the legalist covered with blood. It was not until almost midnight that, ceding to reproofs, he made up his mind to trace the letters of his name at the bottom of the sheet of paper. He got no further than the second letter: the troops of the Convention burst in and a pistol shot broke Robespierre's jaw, his blood staining the document. The gendarme Merda was to boast of having fired the shot and for a while History was to extend merit to his picturesque name.

The following day, twenty-two condemned prisoners were led to the guillotine, moved back to Place de la Concorde for the occasion. Robespierre was the twentieth and the mayor Fleuriot, the last. With his head, the Commune of Paris also fell. The next day the club of the Jacobins was arrested. Another eighty-three Robespierrists went to the scaffold in the days to follow: the worst hecatomb of the Revolution.

The Thermidor reaction — The Thermidorians, still surprised by their victory, now found themselves in the lead, carried along by a strong reactionary current which called for the opening of the prisons, freedom of thought and action, the reopening of the churches. In the streets, the first Incroyables (dandies), in stylish tail-coats, their hair in bangs, cravats with three turns and weighted sticks hunted down the Jacobins.

In this atmosphere of liberation, the Convention made the mistake of suppressing the law of the Maximum (December 24, 1794), and prices at once ran wild, resulting in a food shortage. The profiteers of Thermidor, called Full Bellies (Ventres pourris), were confronted by the Empty Bellies, spurred on by hunger. On 12 Germinal (April 1, 1795) the inhabitants of Faubourg Saint-Antoine invaded the Convention which immediately retaliated by deporting twenty Montagnards, including Billaud-Varennes and Collot d'Herbois.

The revolt of 1 Prairial — A new revolt instigated by hunger flared up on 1 Prairial. The Convention was once more assaulted and the head of the deputy Féraud ended up on the tip of a pike. This time the survivors of the Montagnards got the upper hand, took control of the Assembly, decreed the Terror and... went to bed.

How they could have been this foolhardy, after six years experience, is hard to understand. During the night, the Thermidorians once more took over the hall, the Convention went back into session and voted the arrest of the Montagnards, and, for the first time since 1789, abrogated the edict which forbade the infantry from entering the capital. The day after, the soldiers arrived commanded by 25-year-old generals, and attacked the Faubourg Saint-Antoine. The rioters tried to parley with the dragoons, one of whom replied:

— When I am on duty, I parley only with my saber.

The armed forces became the arbiters: soon they became the masters.

The repression, once more, was terrible. The prison gates were opened to swallow up five thousand Jacobins, or purported such, and an edict ordered the destruction of their clubs. After which the Convention was free to elaborate and promulgate a new constitution specifying that two thirds of the new deputies were to be re-elected, unpopular as they might be, from the old Convention, the members of which were thus left to nominate themselves.

The Royalist insurrection — The Royalists believed they could turn the torrent of indignation aroused by this provision to their advantage. The sections of the center, led by what is now the quarter of the Bourse, rose in arms against the Convention and were on the point of prevailing, thanks to the hesitation of General Menou, commander of the troops stationed at the Sablons. But the Assembly was by now used to insurrections — Menou was dismissed and the command was turned over to Barras flanked by Brune and by Bonaparte who liberated the Convention by the use of artillery on 13 Vendémiaire (October 5).

THE DIRECTORY

(October 1795 - November 1799)

During this final period of the Revolution known as the Directory, Paris no longer played a leading, almost exclusive, role in the events as before. After 9 Thermidor the Commune ceased to exist and the Parisians, deluded, sceptical, had all they could do to make ends meet and were no longer interested in rioting. The capital continued to be the stage for the unfolding of internal events, with a mediocre ruling class attempting to solve economic problems (the collapse of the assignats), put down conspiracies (that of Babeuf), and above all retain power despite popular opposition, with a see-sawing of one coup d'etat after another. All set against a background of agiotage, financial intrigue, corruption, with the juxtaposition of an unbridled perverse luxury and a misery which struck widely differing classes of society. The government of the "bourgeois Republic" of the Directors, even though it had achieved a certain financial balance, was discredited as much by its laxism and its corruption as by the blows it struck first at one and then at the other opposition, royalists and neo-Jacobins. The last coup d'etat of the period, that of 18-19 Brumaire, generated the Regime and terminated the Revolution.

△ **Coup d'Etat of 18 Fructidor** (engraving by Berthault, Musée Carnavalet). One of the two ramps built during the Revolution can be seen on the right in this engraving which depicts the arrest of Pichegru and his complices in the Tuileries.

▽ **The Day of 19 Brumaire** (engraving by Helman, Musée Carnavalet). In the Orangerie of Saint-Cloud, Napoleon, threatened by the members of the Council of Five Hundred in costume, is rescued by his Grenadiers.

THE PLACES OF THE REVOLUTION

LE MARAIS - LES HALLES - LES ILES

THE BASTILLE

1

It makes no sense to tell the story of the Bastille once more, unless it is to specify that the fortress was not at all "taken": it surrendered, a fitting symbol of the attitude of the regime. Let it simply be noted that no time was lost in its demolition, coordinated by the picturesque Palloy. Models of the fortress have been preserved, more or less throughout France, as well as ground plans engraved on some of its stones, medals minted with the metal from the prison ironwork... Palloy was to ruin himself with this impartial manufacture of souvenirs.

A fountain called the fountain of Regeneration was soon erected on the spot. It consisted of a statue representing the Nation, vaguely Egyptian in style, with water, which the Convention went in procession to drink, flowing from her breasts. But this ornament was short-lived. The guillotine was erected here from the 9th to 12th of June in 1794.

Yet not every trace of the fortress has disappeared from the Place de la Bastille. The ground plan is depicted on a plaque at number 3 on the square and is to be found, in its actual size, on the paving, where, after the excavations, the outline of the facade with its towers and the curtain walls in between was marked. It will be noted that the square as it is now does not correspond exactly to the site of the fortress, for it is in part occupied by the block that separates the Rue Saint-Antoine from the Boulevard Bourdon, that is the Bank of France, another form of power... The outline of the Tour Coin is visible opposite the bank, on the axis of the Rue Saint-Antoine, before arriving at the square, as well as that of the Tour de la Liberté, and, further on, that of the Tour de la Chapelle, and in front of the houses that of the Tour de Trésor, with the Tour de la Comté on the axis of the Boulevard Bourdon. Not far behind this was the principal drawbridge, at the edge of the current sidewalk.

▷ **The Taking of the Bastille** (J. P. Houel, gouache, Musée Carnavalet). In the foreground, the drawbridge of the Avancée, on the site of what is now Boulevard Henri IV.

△ **Place de la Bastille as it is now.** The outline of the fortress is still visible on the paving of the Place.

▷ **The Demolition of the Bastille** (J. P. Houel, gouache, Musée Carnavalet). The demolition of the fortress was begun the day after July 14th, under the direction of the contracter Palloy who was aided by numerous volunteers. The work was practically finished a year later.

The column stands on the site of the triangular bastion which protected the fort on the east.
Underground in the métro station *Bastille* (line 5), on the platform direction Bobigny, there are remains discovered during the digging of the line, accompanied by records, on the premises, in many respects difficult to decipher. What we have here is the abutment of the fixed bridge, grafted onto the eastern counterscarp of the moat of the fortress, joining the latter to the triangular bastion. On the station platform, a paving indicates the silhouette of this counterscarp. Here we find ourselves opposite the towers of the Trésor and of the Chapelle, exactly on an axis with the east facade of the Bastille.

△ **Model of the Bastille** (Musée Carnavalet). During the demolition of the fortress, Palloy had numerous souvenirs made, including models of the Bastille, either in stone taken from the structure or in plaster.

◁ **The Fountain of Regeneration** (engraving by Helman, Bibliothèque des Arts décoratifs). Set on the site of the fortress, the fountain was inaugurated on August 10 1793 for the anniversary of the fall of the monarchy.

▷ **Vestiges of the Tour de la Liberté of the Bastille**, Square Henri Galli.

▷ **Vestiges of the Bastille** on the platform of the métro.

A few years before, in 1899, the passage of line 1 of the métro, which forms a segmental arc from the Tour de la Comté to the Tour de la Liberté, had brought to light the foundations of the latter: its name, rather odd for a prison, was derived from the fact that it was where privileged prisoners were kept, free to leave their cells for walks in the prison court of honor or the governor's garden. It is said that the Marquis de Sade was imprisoned here.
These vestiges, taken apart stone by stone, were set up 500 meters away in the public gardens of Galli.

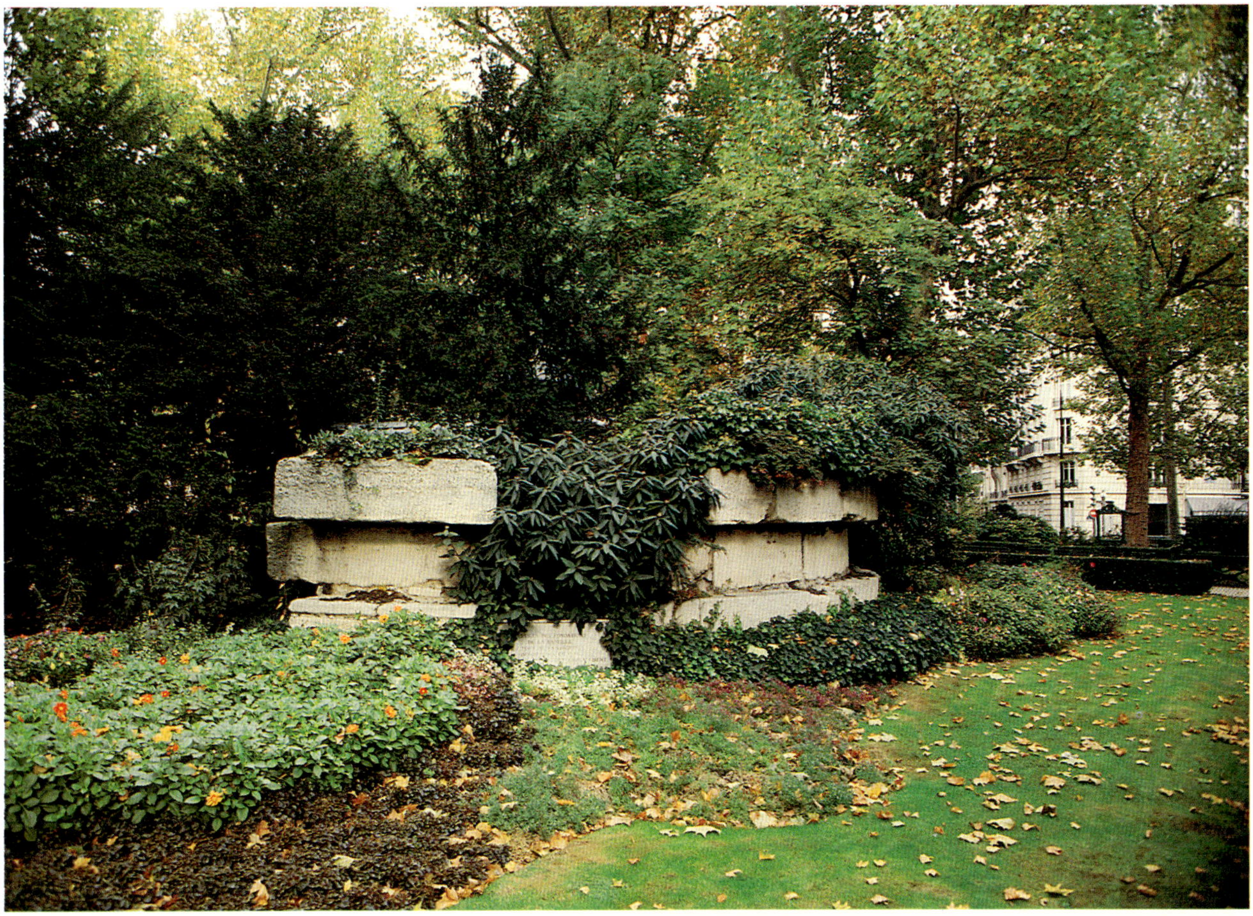

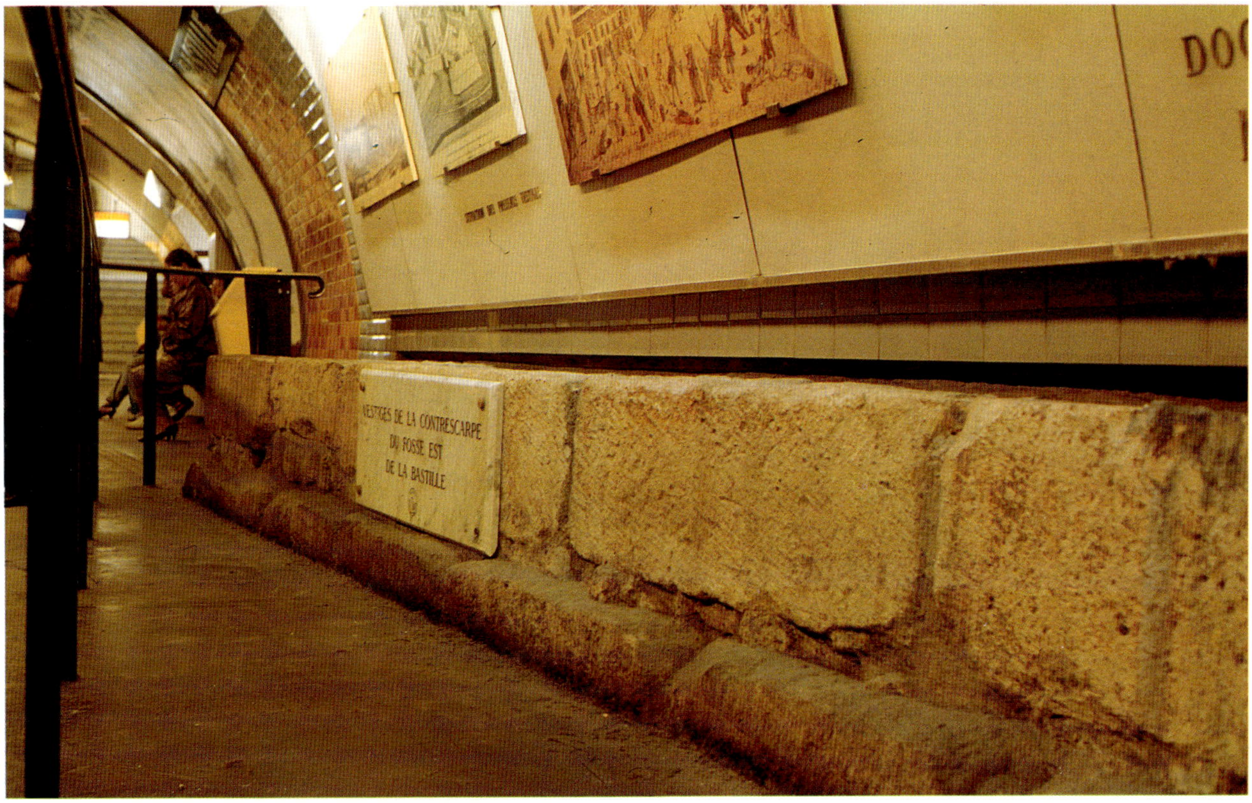
VESTIGES DE LA CONTRESCARPE
DU FOSSE EST
DE LA BASTILLE

2 TEMPLE DE LA VISITATION SAINTE-MARIE
17 rue Saint-Antoine

Suppressed in 1790, the convent was rented to a club. A Phrygian bonnet is still to be seen carved above the old side door on the east as well as the inscription *"Lois et actes de l'Autorité publique"* on the right side of the facade on the Rue Saint-Antoine.

3 ARCADE DE BRETONVILLIERS
Rue de Bretonvilliers

This structure is the greater part of what remains of the grand town house of Bretonvilliers, dating to the 17th century, which was sequestered in 1793 as the property of an *émigré* and became the grand prize of the first national lottery in 1794.

4 THE THEATER OF BEAUMARCHAIS
11 rue de Sévigné

A house known as the Petit Hôtel Lamoignon used to stand here and Beaumarchais, who lived right nearby (Boulevard Beaumarchais now), bought the area around 1790 as site for a theater apparently constructed with stones from the Bastille. It was inaugurated on September 1, 1791 with *La Métromanie* by Piron and on June 26th, Beaumarchais presented the première of *La mère coupable*, last in the series of Figaro's adventures, and it was a flop. The theater disappeared a few years later. The facade, decorated with large pilasters, and ironwork, is still visible.

▽ **Formerly a theater** built by Beaumarchais in the Rue de Sévigné.

LA FORCE
22 rue Pavée

A corner of a wall in vermiculate rustication on one side of the Hôtel Lamoignon (it is the left end of the facade of the "Petite Force") and a high wall to be found at the back of the court of 11 Rue de Sévigné (old enclosing wall of the prison) are all that is left of one of the most famous revolutionary prisons, La Force.

There were actually at the time two buildings for detention, separate but communicating, the Petite Force, in the Rue Pavée next to the Hôtel Lamoignon and reserved for the women, and the Grande Force, south of the former and extending as far as the street baptized in the Revolution as Rue des Droits de l'Homme (Rue du Roi de Sicile). The latter prison can be reached from the Rue Saint-Antoine, through a lane, the Rue des Ballets (situated at the end of the Rue Malher) with a muddy rivulet in the center, flanked by hovels.

From 1792 on, the distinction between the two prisons ceased to be observed and prisoners of both sexes were crowded into the one and the other. After August 10th, a number of friends of the royal family were enclosed there.

When the massacres of September began, various commissaries of the Assembly did all in their power to free those they could, such as, for example, Mme de Tourzel and her daughter, but the Princess de Lamballe, interned after August 19th, stayed there.

On September 2nd, a "tribunal" composed of ten men was installed in the clerk's office of the Grand Force. They were assisted by five "*travailleurs*" (laborers) stationed at the entrance to the prison who, armed with cudgels, killed the condemned as they crossed the threshold. The dead bodies were despoiled and piled up by the "*deplayeurs*" (cleaners-up) who received wages of twenty-four *livres* for their work, which they had obtained through Billaud-Varennes. Stationed at the entrance to the prison, the painter David cooly sketched the corpses as they piled up.

▽ **The Capital Punishment of Mme de Lamballe on September 3, 1790** (engraving, Cabinet des Estampes). In the foreground, massacre of the priests of the Carmes. In the background, a group of insurgents on their way to the Temple, with the head of the Princess de Lamballe stuck on a pike.

The Princess de Lamballe, after a mock interrogation, was dismissed with the words: Madame may freely go, and she was led to the door where at the sight of the corpses piled high she cried: — *Fi, L'horreur*! These were her last words. Overpowered, cut down by a rain of blows, she was denuded and left naked for two hours on the pavement. Her corpse was then dragged to the corner of the Rue des Droits de l'Homme and Rue des Ballets, where there was a cornerstone on which a certain Grison cut off her head with his knife and impaled it on a pike (at present southwest corner of the intersection Roi de Sicile-Malher, in front of the Prénatal department store). Her heart was wrenched from her breast and her body was subjected to other obscene mutilations. The head was taken in procession, along the Boulevard Beaumarchais, as far as the Temple and the Palais Royal. The depths of ignominy and uncalled - for acrimony reached here make this one of the most sinister episodes in a Revolution that already had more than its share.

The exact number of victims is not known — certainly more than a hundred.

Then the prison was once more filled, first with common law prisoners, then with *suspects*, but under a compliant regime. A famous chef had set up shop next door and supplied those prisoners who could pay with the most refined meals, that were followed by tranquil games of whist, piquet or chess.

In practice everything was permitted at La Force in that period, except leaving it, and even here "permissions" were granted: Cambon, the finance minister, had Garat, an employee of the Treasury, brought to him almost every day, escorted by two gendarmes, so they could work together, and in the evening he had him reaccompanied to La Force. The wives of the prisoners took up lodgings nearby and during their visits, often managed to go off with them in private.

The atmosphere changed with the "prison plot" in May of 1794. From then on, every evening, a bell tolled to announce the arrival of the bailiff of the revolutionary Tribunal, bringing the list, drawn up by Fouquier-Tinville, of those who were to appear before the judges the next day.

Among the prisoners who left La Force for the guillotine mention can be made of the Maréchal de Noailles, the advocate Linguet, Baron de Trenck, eternal prisoner, thirteen Girondin deputies including Vergniaud, the former mayor Bailly etc... On the other hand, Choderlos de Laclos, Ledoux, the picturesque General Miranda, Maréchal de Ségur, Mlle Montansier, the writer Volney were let free.

It was from La Force, on 7 Thermidor, that Thereza Cabarrus, imprisoned by order of Robespierre, sent her lover Tallien this famous and cutting note:

"The police administrator is leaving; he came to tell me that, tomorrow, I am to go on the Tribunal, that is to the scaffold. This bears little resemblance to the dream I had last night: Robespierre no longer existed and the prisons had been opened... But thanks to your illustrious

▽ **Death of Mme de Lamballe on September 3, 1792**
(engraving, Cabinet des Estampes).

△ **Extant remains of the prison of La Force.** This section of decorated wall was part of the facade of the Petite Force. On the left, the Hôtel Lamoignon.

△ **The house at 113 Boulevard Beaumarchais.** This was where the head of the Princess de Lamballe was washed before being taken to the Temple.

dastardliness, there will soon be no one left in France capable of realizing my dream".
This lashing was to play a determining role in the preparation of 9 Thermidor. On that day, Augustin Robespierre and Le Bas were momentarily shut up here, before being liberated by the Commune. After that the history of the double prison came to a halt: it was to be demolished fifty years later.

6 HOUSE

113 boulevard Beaumarchais

In front of this house, built in 1773, the butchers of the prison of La Force stopped to wash the head of the Princess de Lamballe, which they were carrying at the top of a pike, in a pail used for watering horses before taking it to the Temple keep.

7 ANCIEN THÉÂTRE

117 rue Vieille de Temple

The theater was intensely active during the Revolution and even in the worst days of the Terror, they were going strong and very popular: the Parisians were trying to forget, and to live. In the beginning of 1791 the monopoly of the three State theaters, Opéra, Comédie française and Comédie italienne was abolished and numerous playhouses were opened. Thousands of pieces were performed. Only a few vestiges of these new halls have been preserved: the facade of the theater of Beaumarchais, Rue de Sévigné, the one in the former church of the Recollettes and the one found here in 1970. Of timber, it had several tiers of circles. This may have been the famous *Boudoir des musés*, often mentioned in the press of the time.

THE TEMPLE
Square du Temple

Nothing remains to show us what the quarter of the Temple looked like at the end of the 18th century: the keep, the Hôtel du Grand Prieur, the church, the rotunda and the wall itself have all disappeared. The public gardens there now date to the Second Empire. A study of the large plan incised in marble at the corner of the Rue Dupetit-Thouars and the Rue Gabriel Vicaire in which the old structures and the modern streets are superimposed convincingly confirms this drastic change. The "*grosse tour*" of the temple, built at the end of the 13th century, was on the site of the Rue Eugène Spuller, between the public gardens and the town hall of the III *arrondissement*. Here the royal family was shut up on August 13, 1792, in the custody of Santerre, commander of the National Guard, who allowed the prisoners out every day for walks in the garden: the Dauphin could play ball or quoits. It is said that Louis XVI used to read sitting on a small rock grotto which is now in the garden of the town hall of Neuilly.

During these walks, various newshawks approached the enclosing wall, crying out the latest news. This is how the king learned of the massacre of September 2nd. On the 3rd, a group of rioters tried to show the head of the Princess de Lamballe stuck on a pike to the queen through a window: Clery succeeded in sparing her this spectacle.

The day after the massacre, the walks were suppressed. Louis XVI remained locked up here until the day of his execution, January 21, 1793, leaving only for the trial; Marie Antoinette until August 1, 1793, when she was transferred to the Conciergerie, Mme Elisabeth until May 10, 1794, the day of her execution; the Dauphin until June 8, 1795, the date of his presumed death; Mme Royale until December 18, 1795 (27 Primaire year IV), when she was exchanged by the Directory for French prisoners who had been taken by the Austrians. On July 3, 1793, the Dauphin was placed under the surveillance, apparently benevolent, of the shoemaker Simon and his wife, but they resigned at the end of the sixth month, without stating why, an attitude which has given rise to any number of legends. In the same period, Hébert came almost daily to the Temple, in particular to get the Dauphin, who had

▷ **The Keep of the Temple, Shortly before its Demolition** (Musée Carnavalet).

▽ **The Temple Enclosure, reconstructed View** (engraving, Musée Carnavalet). The keep appears in the background.

38

△ **Prison doors from the Temple** now in the keep of Vincennes.

△ **Vestige of the Madelonnettes.** The large section of wall on the left is all that remains of the prison.

◁ **Louis XVI and his Family Imprisoned in the Keep of the Temple** (engraving, Cabinet des Estampes).

◁ **Louis XVI and his Family Being Transferred to the Temple** (engraving by Berthault, Musée Carnavalet). The house of the Grand Prieur, where the royal family dined the first night, before being imprisoned in the keep, can be seen in the background.

been made drunk, to sign an abject deposition against his mother. After the departure of Simon, the child was shut up in his cell, which soon became a stifling den.
Suspicious of the political influence of pilgrimage sites, Napoleon had the keep of the Temple razed to the ground, just as he had had the Jacobin club demolished. Nothing remains of the former except two cell doors reinstalled in the keep of Vincennes. The site has been totally transformed, and even the weeping willow planted by the Duchess of Angoulême during the Restoration no longer exists.

9 LES MADELONNETTES

6-8 rue de Fontaines du Temple

Turning into the Rue des Fontaines du Temple, across from the west side of the public gardens of the Temple (note on the corner, the pendentive vault with sculptured elements and the old inscription of the name of the street), there is a very ordinary stretch of wall which should be marked by a plaque: it is all that remains of the old convent of the Madelonnettes (Daughters of Magdalen), founded in 1620 by some "repentant" prostitutes, and which extended northwards as far as the Rue du Vertbois.
Closed in 1790, the convent was converted into a prison in 1793, and was soon overcrowded, with prisoners lying in corridors filled with the stench of filthy latrines, others in insect-ridden cells with four rows of three pallets. Among the prisoners, the Abbot Barthelemy, author of the *Voyage du jeune Anacharsis*, Chamfort, the Marquis de La Tour du Pin, respectively former minister of war and minister of the navy, a civil lieutenant and a police lieutenant, as well as thirteen actors of the Théâtre français who had remained loyal to the ancien régime. Some of these prisoners left for the guillotine, but in 1794 the survivors were transferred to other prisons, when the Madelonnettes became a prison for common law criminals, which it remained until it was torn down in 1868.

10 CONSERVATOIRE DES ARTS ET MÉTIERS

292 rue Saint-Martin

What we have here is one of the most important and lasting creations of the Revolution. On August 15 and 18 of 1793 the Convention charged the Committee of Public Instruction with selecting significant examples of objects that were related to the arts, the sciences and the crafts from the enormous accumulation of material that had been confiscated by the Nation. Thanks to the decisive action of the Abbot Grégoire and the physicist Charles, a collection of eight hundred pieces housed in the old town house of the dukes of Aiguillon, Rue de l'Université, led to the creation of the Conservatory of Arts and Crafts there on 19 Vendémiaire year II (October II, 1794). Thanks, once more, to the Abbot Grégoire, a decision of 26 Floréal year VI (May 16, 1798) transferred it to the old priory of Saint-Martin des Champs where it was installed on 12 Germinal year VII (April 2, 1799). The Revolution thus turned an idea broached by Descartes a century and a half before into reality, organizing courses which would permit workers to improve by providing them with exemplary tools.

11 INTERSECTION RUE DE CLÉRY - BOULEVARD SAINT-DENIS

When Louis XVI was called up for trial, they led him from the Temple to the Tuileries by way of the boulevards, and on the way he displayed an interest in the transformation taking place in the city. On January 21, 1793, the day of his execution, he covered the same route, and this was the intersection where Baron de Batz was to make an attempt to liberate him. The other conspirators were the Marquis de La Guiche, the Marquis de Pons, the Prince of Saint-Mauris and the Count de Marsan, whose home in the Rue de Cléry was to be the king's hiding place. Between five and six hundred Royalists were to take part in the operation, but the plot was discovered, no one knows how. Only a few of the conspirators succeeded in reaching the rendezvouz and three were killed in the square while Batz managed to escape.

12 PLACE DU CAIRE

On 24 Vendémiaire year VIII (October 16, 1799) Napoleon had returned to Paris from Egypt, and the Directory was tottering. This famous house in Egyptian style is customarily dated to this period for the decoration of the facade, naive and awkward as it may seem, reveals the architect Berthier's thorough acquaintance with Egyptian art, particularly of the later period. It is both an odd example of the Egyptian taste which was then becoming popular, and the last building in Paris built during the Revolution.

▽ **The refectory of Saint-Martin des Champs**. In 1798 it became the Conservatoire des Arts et Métiers, and is still used as such.

△ **Funeral Obsequies for Mirabeau at the church of Saint-Eustache on April 4, 1791** (engraving by Berthault, Cabinet des Estampes).

13 CHURCH OF SAINT-EUSTACHE

The funeral of Mirabeau was celebrated here on April 3, 1791. The entire National Guard in active duty attended and a salvo of twenty thousand rifle shots was fired in the church: those present thought the vault was falling and almost two thousand panes were broken. It is said that a hundred thousand people followed the funeral procession. In 1793 the church was closed, pillaged and sacked and then reopened in 1795. Part of it was turned over, from 1797 to 1802, to the Théophilanthropes, under the name of Temple of Agriculture.

14 THE COUR BATAVE

60 rue Saint-Denis

In 1791 a group of Dutch merchants bought the old convent of the Holy Sepulcher, situated between the Rue Saint-Denis, Rue Aubry le Boucher, Rue de Venise and Rue Quincampoix. It had been suppressed the year before, and they had it torn down. On this vast empty area the architects Sobre and Happe built what was then known as the Cour Batave (at the time Holland was known as Batavia), a complex of business and representational buildings consisting of two successive courtyards surrounded by galleries of shops, access to which was through vaulted passageways framed by Ionic columns. At the back of the second courtyard a niche containing a fountain of plenty was flanked by two lions.

The opening of the Boulevard Sébastopol and the extension of the Rue de la Cossonnerie were fatal to this complex, but a vestige still remains in a building at 60 Rue Saint-Denis, where the decoration is still almost intact: the lion heads, the balconies in wrought iron, the antique friezes.

PLACE DE GRÈVE
Place de l'Hôtel de Ville

A particularly popular site, the Place de Grève was to play a determining role throughout the Revolution. Even though the city hall of the time has disappeared completely (the central part of the present building is a copy) and the square, considerably enlarged, has been totally transformed, some of the principal events which took place here can be evoked.

The first riots date to 1789, and it was here that Bertier de Sauvigny, *intendant* of Paris, accused, with his father-in-law Foulon, of having starved the people in order to maintain the foreign troops, was massacred by the mob. Since the last provost of the tradesmen had also been assassinated, a new *municipalité*, presided over by the astronomer Bailly, took over the day after the fall of the Bastille, and received Louis XVI on July 27th. Bailly, responsible for the shooting in the Champ de Mars, was dismissed at the beginning of the Legislative Assembly and replaced by Pétion.

The Marquis de Favras, accused of plotting the assassination of Necker, La Fayette and Bailly, as well as the abduction of the king, was, after an iniquitous trial, condemned to the gallows, the first application of the equality of the penalty. The execution took place here on February 17, 1790 and an assistant cried: — *Saute, marquis*! (Jump, marquis!).
The phrase was to remain famous.

And it was here that the guillotine made its first appearance, on April 25, 1792, to execute a certain Pelletier, condemned for theft and nocturnal aggression. Up to the end of the Terror those condemned by common law, and only those, were to be executed in this spot.

▽ **Louis XVI on his Way to the Hôtel de Ville on July 17, 1789** (optical view, Bibliothèque des Arts décoratifs).

△ **The Hôtel de Ville as it is today.** The central part of the facade is modelled on the building that existed during the Revolution and which disappeared in 1871.

An insurrectional Commune had occuped the Hôtel de Ville the morning of August 10th and the assassination of Mandat, on the steps of the town hall was the starting signal for the last assault on the monarchy. From then on, the illegal Commune, responsible for the captivity of the royal family, was to play a determining role until the Comité de Salut public (Committee of Public Safety) gradually regained power.

In November 1793, a band of rioters entered the church of Sainte-Geneviève next to Saint-Etienne du Mont, and profanated the shrine of saint. At first they hesitated in front of the reliquary studded with a thousand precious stones, which was sent to the Mint. . . where the gems turned out to be fakes. Perhaps in an attempt to get even, on November 21st they carried the "bones and worthless rags" found in the reliquary out into the square in Place de Grève and publicly burned them, throwing the ashes into the Seine.

Then the Terror gathered momentum: between 26 Prairial (June 14, 1794) and 9 Thermidor (July 27), every day except the decade (every 10th day), late in the afternoon the procession of condemned prisoners, tumbrils surrounded by an escort on foot and on horseback, crossed the square.

The last act of the day of 9 Thermidor was played at the Hôtel de Ville, which witnessed the end of the great insurrectional movement which had been born there. On 10 Thermidor (July 28), around two thirty in the morning, the troops of the Convention took over the building without resistance: Robespierre was wounded by a mysterious pistol shot, which he himself may have fired, his brother threw himself out the window, Lebas blew out his

△ **The Hôtel de Ville before the Revolution** (N. Raguenet, painting, Musée Carnavalet). Built during the Renaissance, it stood on the site of the central part of the present city hall. On the right, the church of Saint-Jean-en-Grève. In the foreground, the Place de Grève.

brains, Coffinhal, having grabbed Hanriot by the collar, threw him out of another window and for the time being managed to flee, Couthon dragged himself under a table where he was discovered and thrown down the stairs. The wounded were rounded up and sent on their way to the guillotine, as was the mayor Fleuriot-Lescot. This was the end of the hegemony of the Commune of Paris.

Lastly on May 6, 1795, it was in Place de Grève that before an immense raging crowd Fouquier-Tinville and some of the most jeopardized jurors or prison-spies were executed. The knife fell sixteen times.

16 TOUR SAINT-JACQUES
Square Saint-Jacques

In 1790 the large church of Saint-Jacques La Boucherie was closed to worship and in 1793 the revolutionary committee ''of the Lombards'' toppled the large statue of Saint Jacques from the top of the tower. On October 26, 1797, the church was sold at auction, but on the condition that the tower remain standing. The church was destroyed, and the tombstone of Nicolas Flamel, bought by a greengrocer, was used as a chopping board for his greens.

The tower was bought by a Mr. Dubois, who made shot for hunters: he had the melted metal pass through the tubes of a boiler which reduced it to drops which fell, at the bottom of the tower, into large tubs of water.

◁ **Foulon Hanged in the Place de Grève on July 23, 1789** (Prieur, drawing, Musée Carnavalet). He was afterwards beheaded.

◁ **The Troops of the Convention Attacking the Hôtel de Ville the Night of 9 to 10 Thermidor** (engraving by Helman, Musée Carnavalet).

▷ **The Tour Saint-Jacques as it is today.**

PALAIS DE JUSTICE
Boulevard du Palais

Very little remains of what those accused by the Revolution and called to appear before the Tribunal saw, what with the reconstruction of the Palais in the Second Empire and the fire of 1871. On their arrival from the Conciergerie, the men mounted the staircase of the Tour Bonbec, the women the steps of the Tour de la Chapelle, and crossed, on the first floor, rooms that have now been transformed except for the *galerie marchande* and the prisoners' corridor, which have retained their lovely Louis XVI architecture with Doric columns and pediments carved with emblems. From there they were led, avoiding the Grande Salle up to the Grand Chambre, where the fine coffered Louis XII ceiling had been covered. In 1785-86 the trial of Cardinal de Rohan was held here, the first affront to the monarchy: here, in 1788, the king tried in vain to make Parlement yield to his will. But this victory was short-lived, for the revolutionary Tribune, created on March 10, 1793, and composed of mediocre and corrupt men, governed by hate of the past, in the grasp of a summary and dramatic Manicheism, set up its headquarters in this room in the heart of the palace.

"High-flown Revolutionary ridicule", wrote J. J. Leveque, "may have been attained in this spot". All the great trials of the period took place in this room, now the First Chamber of the Civil Court. Between the 6th of April 1793 and the 10th of June 1794, a period of 430 days, 1251 death sentences were meted out. Between the 11th of June and the 27th of July, 1794, a period of 43 days, 1376 were issued.

After 1871, Duc and Daumet attempted an unconvincing restoration in Louis XII style. The only thing remaining is the spot where Marie Antoinette, when faced with the base accusations of Hébert and Fouquier-Tinville, exclaimed — I appeal to all the mothers who are here!

▷ **The Palais de Justice during the Revolution** (Senave, Musée Carnavalet). At the center, the Sainte-Chapelle and the windows of the Grand'Salle (Salle des Pas Perdus). On the right, la Tour de l'Horloge and, in front, the Pont au Change, over which the procession passed on its way to the guillotine.

▽ **The Mayor of Paris Going to the Palace to Set his Seals on the Acts of Parlement, November 1790** (engraving by Berthault, Musée Carnavalet). View of the Cour du Mai in the Palais de Justice.

CONCIERGERIE

Quai de l'Horloge

The royal palace of the Cité as early as the Middle Ages was placed under the authority of a "concierge" who exercised the right of justice and had a prison at his disposal, which dated to the 13th century. At the beginning of the Revolution, it occupied the entire ground floor of that part of the building which flanked the banks of the river: courtyards for men and for women with adjoining prisons, guard rooms, the lower parts of the three towers of the facade and the chapel, as well as a sector, called "rue de Paris", in the room of the Gens d'armes.

The first revolutionary episode which took place here was the massacre of the first days of September 1792. As was the case with the same crimes in the other prisons, the responsibility was attributed on one part to the newspapers, which were clamoring for death, notoriously that of Fabre d'Eglantine, and on the other, to the Commune which organized them or kept a *laissez faire* policy, and lastly to Danton, minister of Justice who did nothing to prevent them.

Here, over a period of hours, the murderous mob invaded the corridors and the dungeons of the old prison, pursued the prisoners, there for common crimes, and the cries of hate with which they incited each other mingled with the screams of their victims. In the women's section, on the contrary, they freed all the prisoners, except the "flower vender of the Royal Palace" who was brutally tortured. Chabot, a former Capuchin monk and member of the Convention, was delegated by the Assembly to halt the massacres in the prisons, but did nothing, declaring "the justice of the people could not be arrested".

When this storm had passed, a few months later the Conciergerie became a legal machine for slaughter, in function round the clock. The prisoners brought here to appear before the revolutionary Tribunal were taken off the wagon in the Cour de Mai and led, on the right, to a small courtyard at a lower level controlled by a guard situated under the stairs. At the back of this courtyard were the wicket gates consisting of two successive doors which led to an atrium, at present the palace buffet. To the left were two rooms, the clerk's office where the registers of arrivals was kept, and the back office where the prisoners were stripped of most of what they had.

The different parts of the prison were all reached from the atrium. The men were sent to the various rooms around the men's courtyard (Cour des Hommes): those who had a little money to the "*quartiers des pistoliers*" (as paying "guests") to the west of the courtyard and facing the Seine, between the Tour d'Argent and the Tour Bonbec. The prisoners who had nothing were crowded into the quarter of the Pailleux, east of the courtyard, in the guards' room divided into two floors by planking, or in the "rue de Paris", the old sector of the room of the Gens d'armes, a narrow unlit passageway, infested by rats and where under the Terror as many as two hundred and fifty prisoners were kept stretched out on a veritable mass of dung. The women were sent, at the back of the

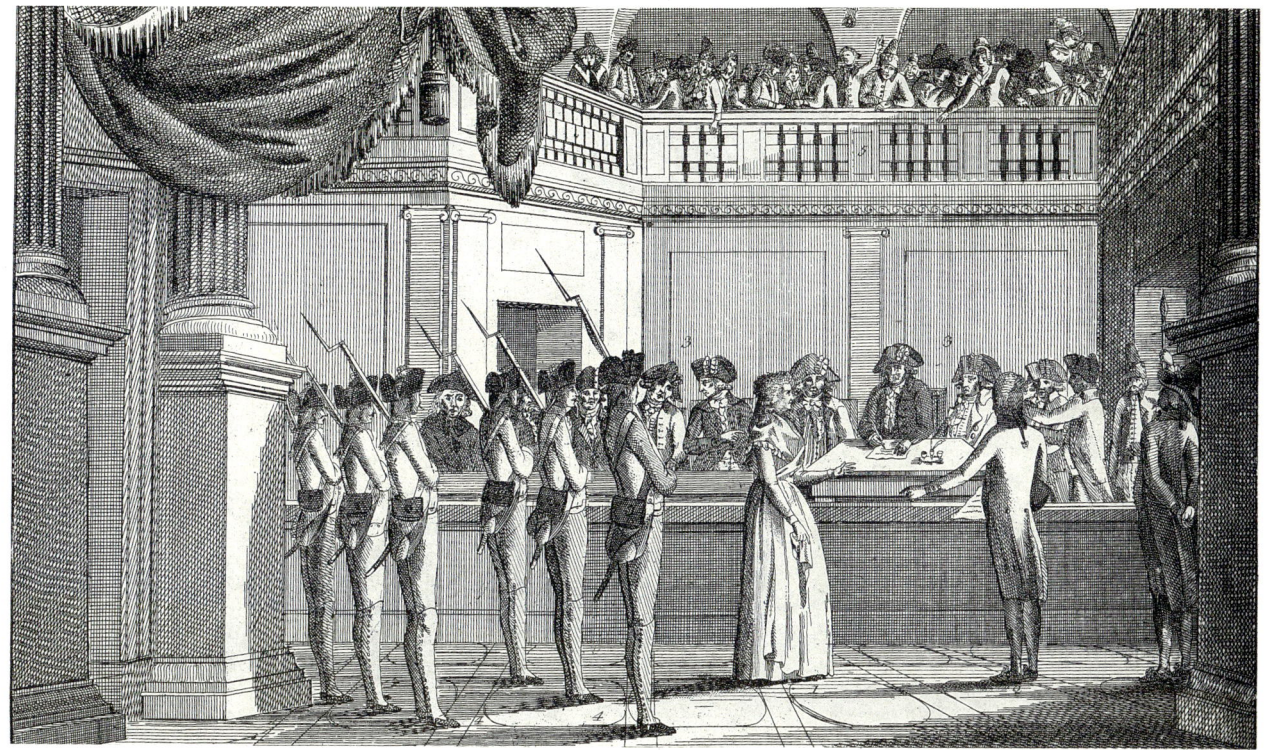

△ **Trial of Marie Antoinette** (engraving, Musée Carnavalet).

▷ **Cell door from the Conciergerie** (Sceaux, Musée de l'Ile-de-France).

◁ **The Conciergerie as it is today.** Fouquier-Tinville's offices were on the first floor of the twin towers, de César and d'Argent, on the right.

atrium, to the prisons arranged around the Cour des Femmes: dormitories strewed with filthy straw on the ground floor, separate cells on the first floor.

While they were in prison, generally not very long for the Conciergerie was the antechamber to the guillotine, the prisoners were authorized, in certain hours, to walk in their respective courtyards. That of the women was provided with a fountain, still there, where they could wash their lingerie, and it was separated by a grating (no longer in its original place) from a small courtyard used by the men: numerous reunions or intrigues took place through these bars.

Every evening, at the foot of the small spiral staircase flanking the Tour Bonbec, the list of prisoners called to appear before the Tribunal the next day was read. When the time came, with faltering step those named climbed the stairs up to the audience hall above the guard room. The women went by the chapel staircase.

When the sentence had been pronounced, generally around the middle of the afternoon, the prisoners were taken back to the Conciergerie, but not to their old cell. The men were crowded into the back office, the women in one or the other of the small dark dungeons behind the atrium. Here they waited, sometimes as long as thirty-six hours, for the guillotine was not in function on the decades (tenth days).

When the executioner and his helpers arrived, the condemned prisoners were gathered together in the "*salle de*

△ **The Conciergerie, the women's wing:** the corridor leading to the cells.

△ **The Conciergerie, Chapel of the Girondins.** The Girondin deputies condemned to death passed their last night here.

la toilette", to the right of the atrium. Here they were searched and stripped of whatever they might still have, then turned over to Sanson's helpers, who set the prisoners on stools, made an ample cut in the neck of their shirts and cut off their hair, level with the nape, which then became the property of the headsmen.

Men and women were then led, through doors and small courts, to the Cour de Mai, where the tumbril was waiting for them and on which they haltingly climbed, under the hail of cries from the "*furies de la guillotine*" who were stationed on the steps of the palace. The tumbrils, bearing ten persons each and escorted by gendarmes on foot and on horseback, left the Cour du Mai, turned left in the Rue de la Barillerie (Boulevard du Palais), crossed the Pont au Change, the Place du Chatelet and then turned left or right, depending on whether the guillotine was set up in Place de la Révolution or Place du Trône renversé, continuing in the dying sun this long journey of death.

The terrible law of Prairial accellerated the movement, and thereafter, there were about fifty death sentences per day. Thus more than two thousand prisoners passed here between 1793 and 1795, sometimes staying no more than a few hours. To cite only the most outstanding, Charlotte Corday (the door thought to come from her cell is now in the Musée de l'Île de France, in Sceaux) and, on August 2, 1793, Marie Antoinette.

The queen was initially shut up in a cell near the entrance where the Chevalier de Rougeville managed to pass her a carnation in which he had hidden a note that announced preparations for her escape. But an imprudence on the part of Marie Antoinette led to the discovery of the "carnation conspiracy" and on September 4th the prisoner was transferred to another cell, strictly guarded day and night. She was brought back there on October 16th at four in the morning after being condemned and at the end of the morning led towards the waiting tumbril.

The Girondins, Mme Roland, Philippe Egalité also passed through here. Then at the height of the Reign of Terror, Hébert and the "*enrages*", Danton and his friends including Camille Desmoulins, Hérault de Séchelles and Fabre d'Eglantine, later Chaumette, Mme du Barry, Lavoisier, Mme Elisabeth, André Chénier. At that time Mme Hébert, the "Mère Duchesne", a former nun, met Lucile Desmoulins here. Their husbands had been enemies, but they were dead and the two widows were bound by a common destiny. They sat next to each other in the courtyard and wept together. They were both executed on April 13, 1794 (24 Germinal year II).

This machine for killing, functioning day in day out, required frantic work on the part of the man who directed it down to the last detail, the public prosecutor Fouquier-Tinville, nominated in March 1793 and with a salary of 8000 *livres*. He spent fifteen hours a day in his offices on the first floor of the tours de Cesar and d'Argent and in the connecting corridor and left every evening to go and ask for his ration of heads at the Tuileries, from the Comité de Sureté générale, later the Comité de Salut public, before returning to his lodgings situated on the two floors of the tour Bonbec and the common attic. Once as he crossed the Pont au Change on his way back he grasped the arm of his companion and pointed to the Seine: - Look how red it is. . .

On 9 Thermidor he felt the wind was changing and ran to the Convention to assure the masters of the moment of his compliance. Barras then took malicious pleasure sending him his former masters to the Conciergerie: Robespierre, Saint-Just, Couthon, Hanriot, and the president of the Tribunal himself, Dumas. Declared outlaws, they did not have to pass before the judges and after a simple "identification" left directly for the guillotine.

But on 14 Thermidor, as he was drinking a glass of brandy at the bar, Fouquier-Tinville learned that the Convention had emanated an order for his arrest. An hour later, he delivered himself up. "His entrance", wrote Lenôtre, "unleashed a sort of revolt: the prison guard barely had time to throw him into a dark cell and lock the door, and throughout the night, the ex-public prosecutor, to whom just the day before no one had dared raise their eyes, heard the crowd of prisoners beating against the door, overwhelming him with a rain of sarcasm and insults". He had a real trial which lasted thirty-nine days, at the end of which he was guillotined on May 7, 1795. The revolutionary Tribunal was suppressed three weeks later.

In the 19th century various lamentable changes were carried out in the prison of the Conciergerie. The area of the Cour des Hommes still exists but the setting has entirely disappeared for in 1868 the surrounding buildings with their fine Gothic arcading were destroyed. On the other hand, the Cour des Femmes with its fountain and the stone slab is still there, as are the bell which marked the hours for the prison activities, the barred windows of the "*chambres a la pistole*" and the courtyard of the Pailleux. The 18th-century chapel where the Girondins passed their last night (30-31 October 1793) and a certain number of cells can also still be seen. Unfortunately under the Restoration Marie Antoinette's cell was turned into a commemorative chapel. The door has been moved and the entrance is where the queen's bed once stood. The altar is set against a wall that replaces a light partition that separated the cell from a closet where the gendarmes were permanently on guard. The only thing that still looks as it did then is the floor. The adjacent cell where Robespierre passed his last hours is also still there.

▽ **The Girondin Deputies Brought before the Revolutionary Tribunal** (engraving by Duplessis-Bertaux, Musée Carnavalet). They cross the Grand'Salle of the Palais de Justice, now the Salle des Pas Perdus.

PONT-NEUF

The nation was declared in danger on July 12, 1792. It was on the terreplein of the Pont-Neuf, next to the statue of Henry IV, a popular rendezvous for all, that a table was set up on trestles, surrounded by guards beating their drums calling for enlistment: the scene has been popularized in contemporary as well as later prints. Not long after (August 12, 1792), not even the statue of Henry IV was spared in the destruction of the royal statues. Only the slaves flanking the base were saved and are now in the Louvre.

On 10 Thermidor, Robespierre and his friends, taken at the Hôtel de Ville and initially imprisoned in the Tuileries, were moved to the Conciergerie. The Incorruptible, who had been wounded, was carried in an armchair by four men. They stopped to catch their breath in front of the base where the statue had once stood and the fallen tribune, seeing the crowds around the procession, quite visibly shrugged his shoulders.

▷ **The Pont-neuf as it is today**.

◁ **Jousting on the Seine in Memory of the General Federation on July 18, 1790** (Prieur, drawing, Musée Carnavalet).

△ **Recruiting of the National Guard in September 1792** (Léon Cogniet, Musée de Versailles, retrospective tableau). In the background, pedestal of the statue of Henry IV. On the right, the recruiting office.

△ **The Pont-neuf before the Revolution** (N. Raguenet, painting, Musée Carnavalet). In the center, the monument to Henry IV by Jean Bologne (Giambologna) which was later destroyed in August 1792, right across from the two houses at the entrance to the Place Dauphine, Mme Roland lived in the one on the left as a young girl.

THE LOUVRE, THE QUARTER OF THE PALAIS ROYAL AND THE GRANDS BOULEVARDS

△ **Louis XVI on his Way to the Hôtel de Ville on July 17, 1789** (J. P. Houel, Musée Carnavalet). The royal coach is passing along the quay of the Seine, in front of the palace of the Louvre.

▷ **The Grande Galerie in the Louvre** (Hubert Robert, painting, Musée du Louvre). In 1795 the painter was nominated as one of the curators of the new museum. The painting reveals how successful this new institution was.

THE LOUVRE

The idea of opening the royal collections to the public had been broached for quite some time. It was then initiated under Louis XVI by the Comte d'Angiviller, but became reality during the Revolution. The "Museum", officially founded on June 10, 1793, was opened in November of that year in the Salon Carré and the Grande Galerie. Closed for repairs in April 1796, it was reopened in 1799.

But the collections continued to grow, thanks to conquests, despite this temporary closure. Paintings arrived from Belgium in 1794 and as a consequence of the various armistices and treaties (Piacenza, May 9, 1796; Bologna, July 23, 1796; Tolentino, February 12, 1797) the Duke of Parma and the pope had to surrender to France both statues and paintings, the latter put on exhibit in February of 1798. Antique sculpture arrived on July 28th of that same year, and the pieces were installed in Anne of Austria's old apartment on the ground floor which the architect Raymond had adapted for the purpose and where they still are.

▷ **Project for the reorganization of the Grande Galerie of the Louvre** (Hubert Robert, Musée du Louvre). This project was in part carried out one hundred and fifty years later.

PLACE DU CARROUSEL
19

The excavations of the 1980s in the Cour Napoleon have brought to light the tangle of streets which separated the Cour Carrée of the Louvre from the Cour du Carrousel, situated in front of the palace of the Tuileries. This was where Marie Antoinette got lost for two hours on the day of their flight, a delay which was the principal cause of its failure.

The guillotine was set up in Place du Carrousel on August 21, 1792, a few days after the fall of the monarchy. It stayed there (with one exception — the king — until May 1793. It was replaced, on the following August 2nd, by a pyramid dedicated to the memory of Marat, in which was placed the portrait of the Friend of the People, his bathtub, his desk and his lamp. It was situated about fifty meters from the pyramid there now.

◁ **View of the Grande Galerie of the Louvre and the Pont Royal** (J. F. Delpechin, painting, Musée Carnavalet).

▽ **The Arc du Carrousel** today marks the spot where the entrance to the Palais des Tuileries once stood.

PALAIS DES TUILERIES AND GARDENS

Some of the places that recall the period can still be identified on a walk through the gardens.

It must be kept in mind that the palace of the Tuileries was set at right angles to the Seine, between the Pavillon de Flore and that of Marsan. Louis XVI and the royal family lived in this palace from October 6, 1789 to August 20, 1792, with only two interruptions— their summer sojourn to the Château of Saint-Cloud in 1790 and the flight to Varennes, from the 20th to the 25th of June, 1791. During these thirty-four months the king often took walks in the park, at least in the beginning, sometimes accompanied by the Dauphin, for whom a small garden had been installed at the far end of the Tuileries, in the east moat of Place Louis XV, now Place de la Concorde. After their return from Varennes, these walk became rarer.

In October 1789, the Constituent Assembly had followed the king to Paris and on November 9th had taken up headquarters in the hall of the royal riding school (Manège) built for the young Louis XV, which was situated at the north edge of the gardens, on the site of the Rue de Rivoli, between the Rue Saint-Roch and the Rue de Castiglione. A plaque is set in front of 230 Rue de Rivoli, on a pillar which marks the spot where the president of the Assembly had his seat. The hall was at the time anything but suitable, with its elongated proportions and its deplorable acoustics. The king went there several times, in particular to have war on Austria declared.

On August 10, 1792, early in the morning, the palace was stormed, after the Cour du Carrousel, by the mob with cries of "*Déchéance, déchéance!*" and, urged by Roederer, Louis XVI decided to seek protection with the Assembly. Without taking anything, the king and his fa-

▷ **Wallpaper from the room occupied by the Committee of Public Safety**. Reconstruction of the Revolutionary decoration (Sceaux, Musée de l'Ile-de-France).

▽ **The Palace of the Tuileries before the Revolution** (N. Raguenet, painting, Musée Carnavalet). In the background, to the south of the Pavillon de Marsan, the Salle des Machines where the Convention was to meet from 1792 to 1795. In the foreground, the Pavillon de Marsan which was to be the headquarters for the Committee of Public Safety.

△ **The Dagger Affair** (engraving by Berthault, Bibliothèque des Arts décoratifs). The arrest of the Royalist conspirators on February 26, 1791, at the foot of the great staircase of the Tuileries.

mily immediately left the palace through the gardens.
— How early the leaves are falling this year, said the king, treading the dry chestnut foliage underfoot.
Passing near the large basin, they crossed the northeast corner of the gardens, greeted by an occasional cry of — Down with the big pig! and climbed the eleven steps to the terrace of the Feuillants, still to be seen opposite Rue de Castiglione, on their way to the hall of the Manège. Tradition affirms that the young Lieutenant Bonaparte, in the garden just then, saw this pitiful procession pass and expressed his contempt in barracks terminology. He was left with an instinctive horror of the crowd.
After the occupation of the palace, the garden was strewn until the day after with the mutilated bodies of the Swiss guards, observed with curiosity by the women. On the steps of the Pavillon de Flore drunkards were sleeping side by side with the corpses.
The Convention was installed on May 10, 1793 in the Palace of the Tuileries, in the old Salle des Machines that had been suitably adapted. It was to stay there until its last session, on October 26, 1795 (4 Brumaire year IV) and it is therefore here that some of the great Revolutionary episodes of this period unfolded, as for example, the trial of the king, who was condemned to death, right in his own palace, on January 17, 1793, with a single vote of majority, that of the Duc d'Orléans. The hall was south of the present Pavillon de Marsan.
The Committee of Public Safety created by the Convention on April 6, 1793, set up its headquarters in the Pavillon de Flore, replaced by the present pavilion of the same name, and remained there until the day after 9 Thermidor.
During this period, the gardens were the stage for many manifestations, coups de force and fêtes.
On June 2, 1793, the deputies of the Convention with Hérault de Séchelles in the lead, threatened by the troops of Hanriot, attempted to leave through the gardens, but go where they might, they found their way blocked by barriers and riots. In the end they had to reopen their session and turn over the Girondins. A few weeks later, the Revolutionary horse-woman Théroigne de Méricourt was taken by Robespierre's partisans, above all women, who hiked up her clothes and whipped her on the terrace of the Feuillants: as a result she lost her mind. As for the fêtes, the most famous was that of the Supreme Being on 7 Floréal year II (June 8, 1794) over which Robespierre presided. A platform was raised in front of the palace,

△ **The Taking of the Tuileries on August 10, 1792** (J. Bertaux, Musée de Versailles). The Swiss Guards are dressed in red.

◁ **Fête of the Supreme Being in the Tuileries, on 20 Prairial year II** (engraving by Berthault, Musée Carnavalet). On the right, the tribune erected for the Convention in front of the palace of the Tuileries.

◁ **Funeral Ceremony in Honor of Those Who Died on August 10th** (engraving, Musée Carnavalet). The rite takes place in the gardens of the Tuileries, where a pyramid, a favorite funerary motif of the time, has been erected.

◁ **Trial of Louis XVI** (engraving, Musée Carnavalet). The scene shown took place on December 26, 1792 in the hall of the Manège.

from which the Incorruptible delivered a speech in which he presented his theory of "democratic deism" to the crowd which packed the gardens. Then, at the head of the procession he made his way to the central basin, where, on a platform, an enormous pyramidal sculpture of wood and plaster had been constructed, representing Atheism surrounded by Ambition, Egoism, Discord and false Ingenuity, above which floated a banner bearing in capital letteres *Espoir de l'étranger* (hope of the outsider). Robespierre, in an azure gown, carrying a bouquet of immortelles and ears of wheat in one hand and with a torch in the other, set fire to that pile of allegories from which there afterwards emerged a somewhat scorched statue of Wisdom. The procession, which included children wreathed in violets, adolescents in myrtle, women in roses, the men with garlands of oak leaves, the aged with vines and olive leaves, accompanied by the music of Mehul, wended their way to the Champ de Mars.

The fête had been organized by David, who, dressed in an incredible costume, bustled about, waving his hat with its tricolor plume and shouting — Make way! Make way! for the commissary of the Convention!

For the occasion the architect Bernard had designed the two semicircular marble benches decorated with sphinxes which can still be seen on either side of the central avenue.

The same central basin was used on December 10, 1794, when Rousseau's ashes were transferred to the Pantheon. An islet symbolizing the Isle des Peupliers d'Ermenouville where the writer had been buried was set in the center. The coffin passed a night there, illuminated by torches. Several onlookers, imbued with the spirit of Julie or Mme de Warents, went to shed a tear.

But neither for the Romans nor for the Parisians did games take the place of bread, and the dying Convention had potatoes planted in the flower beds bordering the terrace of the Feuillants. This was but a drop in the bucket and, during the days of Prairial, rioters invaded the Assembly and numerous deputies fled through the garden and the terraces, while the Montagne was resuscitated for a few brief hours.

Up until then, the gardens had preserved their well-kept appearance, with flowers and orange trees. But everything changed on 13 Vendémiaire. "This lovely garden", wrote the traveler Meister, "was nothing more than a camp of the wildest kind. All the avenues were full of tents, cannons and half of the large terrace served as a bivouac".

The Consulate put things back into shape and the general layout of the gardens has changed very little in the past two centuries, even though the plants and statues have been renewed. Upon arriving from the western end of the gardens, one can see, on either side of the gates, the sloping ramps installed under the Revolution to provide access to the terraces. From here the people watched the executions until they tired of the spectacle.

▷ **The Day of I Prairial year III at the Convention** (N. S. Maillot, Musée Saint-Denis in Reims). The president Boissy d'Anglas takes off his hat in front of the head of the deputy Féraud, massacred by the rioters.

PALAIS ROYAL

In the last years of the ancien régime the Duc d'Orléans, in need of income, had had a horseshoe-shaped group of buildings constructed on the outskirts of his gardens in the Palais Royal, served by three new streets: Rue de Valois, Rue de Montpensier and Rue de Beaujolais. Designed by the architect Victor Louis, they harmonized in style and had galleries and shops on the ground floor. The garden was public and out of bounds for the police. The place became extraordinarily popular. Cafes, gaming houses, book stalls sprang up and a crowd of newcomers, revelers and teen-agers hung out under the arcades. Masonic lodges, editors of newspapers or of satiric pamphlets and above all intellectual societies which the anglomania of the times sometimes insisted on calling clubs were installed above and in the neighboring streets. One of the best known was the club of Valois, founded by Siezès and installed in the palace itself. From morning to night six thousand people unceasingly moved about in this city within a city. This was the point of departure for manifestos, pamphlets, satirical booklets proposing reforms which jeered at the Court and poured a hail of insults at Marie Antoinette.

All the braggarts in the district, making show of words that were as empty as they were exalting, had rallied round the Duc d'Orléans, who had become famous for his opposition to Louis XVI. He was soon to disappoint them as his fortunes crumbled into dust. Most of those around him were unscrupulous adventurers: Sillery, Liancourt, Noailles, Tilly, Talleyrand, but he had an honest secretary, Choderlos de Laclos, who was charged with drawing up a model of the *Cahiers de doléance* (credentials presented by the deputies with the grievances and instructions of their constituents) which was distributed throughout the parishes of the duke's properties and appanage, and copied in many places. The election of ten deputies of the Nobility of Paris to the estates-general was also prepared, or more precisely, manufactured in the Palais Royal.

After the opening of the estates, the popularity of the Duc d'Orléans was at its height between May and June of 1789. At the Palais Royal Mirabeau, Talleyrand, Laclos tried to interest him in the throne, but to little avail.

On July 11, Louix XVI awkwardly attempted to right the ship of state and dismissed Necker. When the news reached the Palais Royal the day after, the excitable crowd flared up. The young Camille Desmoulins jumped up on a table in front of the Café de Foy, situated at number 57-60 of the arcades of Galerie Montpensier, waving a pistol he had pulled out of this pocket in the air, and cried out:

— Citizens, the dismissal of Necker is the tocsin for a night of St. Bartholomew for the patriots. This very night all the Swiss and German troops will come out of the Champ de Mars and cut our throats: there is only one way out: take up arms.

Enthusiastic and gullible, his listeners adopted a rallying-signal that was to be green, the color of hope: the leaves of the trees in the garden served as their cockades. There was a gallery of wax figures, ancestors of the Musée Grévin, kept by a certain Curtius at number 17 of the Galerie Montpensier: the crowd helped themselves to the busts of the Duc d'Orléans and of Necker and carried them in triumph.

Dramatic events were soon to follw. On July 22nd the

△ **Camille Desmoulins Addressing the Passersby of the Palais Royal on July 11, 1789** (engraving by Berthault, Cabinet des Estampes). The setting has remained practically intact.

◁ **The Palais Royal in 1791** (N. de Lespinasse, drawing, Musée Carnavalet). All around, the buildings erected by the architect Victor Louis between 1781 and 1784. In the center, the Circus, built in 1787-88 and used as a riding school.

▽ **The cannon of the Palais Royal.** Shortly before the Revolution this small cannon was installed in the gardens of the Palais Royal where, struck by the sun, it sounded every day at noon, interrupting the debates for an instant.

head of Foulon, the sixty-four-year old administrator of the armed forces, was taken to the gardens on the tip of a pike, with a fistful of hay in his mouth because he had said, so the story goes:

— If this rabble has no bread, let them eat hay.

"Imagine", was to write Chamfort, "at nine in the evening, in the gardens, between the avenues illuminated with street lamps, all ages, all levels, men and women, mingled and intermixed carefree and lighthearted, for dangers were a thing of the past. Suddenly a new sound is heard, the beating of a drum. Two torches are raised and all eyes are turned. What a sight! A livid bloody head illuminated in a horrible glow! A man advances crying in a lugubrious voice: "Let the justice of the people pass!"

In July 1790, when he returned from a supposed mission to England, Philippe d'Orléans, at this point discredited, found his palace deserted, and gradually liquidated all his possessions. There was however always something going on in the gardens, marked by frequent acts of violence. On May 3, 1791, the pope had defended his rights to Avignon, which the Constituent Assembly had declared annexed. The mob once more went to Curtius, got hold of the bust of the pope and burned it in the gardens. Shortly thereafter, the former Marquis de Saint-Huruge passed over to the Revolution. He let himself be kicked in his seat by the Royalists without protesting:

— I never worry, he said, about what goes on behind me.

The Café Corazza, situated under the arcades from numbers 7 to 12 of Galerie Montpensier, was a beehive of activity. It ended up by becoming a sort of antechamber for the Jacobins.

In July 1792, the deputy Duval d'Esprémény, once well-

know for his opposition to Louis XVI, but later a fervid partisan of the king, was arrested on the terrace of the Feuillants in the Tuileries, dragged to the Palais Royal, and thrown into the central basin. This did not save him from the guillotine. After August 20th, the announcement of la Fayette's desertion resulted in another fire in which his image was burned.

On September 3, 1792, a procession of rioters returning from the Temple, penetrated the palace all the way to where the Duc d'Orléans was supping with Mme de Buffon and presented them with the head of Mme de Lamballe, the prince's sister-in-law.

A few days later, the prince took the name of Philippe Egalité and the Palais Royal became Palais Egalité and its garden the Jardin de la Révolution. Under this infamous nickname, Philippe Egalité, the last in the list, was elected to the convention, and as such, in January 1793, could vote for or against the death of the king. His cowardliness made him vote, on the 17th, for death, and he returned, heavy of heart, to his almost empty palace, replying to Agnes de Buffon when she questioned him from the top of the great staircase:
— I couldn't stand the idea of exile.

A few days later, another regicide, Le Peletier de Sainte-Fargeau, was assassinated by an old bodyguard, Pâris, as he was sitting in the basement of the Café Février.

In the meanwhile, the Palais Royal continued to be the center for all pleasures with cafes, gambling houses, various places of ill fame. Outside the theater of the Palais Royal, spectacles of all sorts were offered to the devotees, such as, for example, for the broadminded souls, that of the "Wild Man", actually a naked blacksmith who abandoned himself in public with a young girl "to the most secret mysteries of Nature", sometimes as many as nineteen shows a day. . . The building at 48 Rue de Valois, still there and famous for its double ramp of stairs, was a house of ill fame, the haunt

△ **Ephigy of the Pope Burned at the Palais Royal on April 6, 1791** (Prieur, drawing, Musée Carnavalet).

▷ **Facade of the Church of Saint-Roch**. It was on these steps that Napoleon fired on the Royalist insurgents on 13 Vendémiaire.

▷ **Day of 13 Vendémiaire** (engraving by Berthault, Musée Carnavalet). On the left, Napoleon's artillery opposite the church of Saint-Roch.

of prostitutes, and with a dangerous gambling house in the nineteen rooms on the ground floor and the mezzanine. Philippe Egalité's comportment reached new levels of abjection and his destiny was drawing to its close. On April 7, 1793, when news of the desertion of his son Louis-Philippe arrived, he was arrested together with his youngest son and taken to the prison of the Abbaye. On his way to the scaffold on November 6th he was to pass for the last time in front of his Palais Royal, abandoned, uncared for, degraded. But in the meantime the garden had been the point of departure for still another event. On July 13th, in arcade 117, Galerie de Valois, a Norman girl had bought a strong carving knife, for two francs, with which she went to see Marat.

Animation in the garden, which had diminished during the Terror, steadily increased after Thermidor. The sans-culottes in their *carmagnoles* were replaced by the *Merveilleuses* in transparent tunics and the dandies with their weighted cudgels who reigned in the cafes. More than ever was going on at the Corazza. Barras, Merlin de Thionville, Talma, and the obscure General Bonaparte could be seen. "The sly little Corsican", Barras was to write, "held forth in the cafe Corazza where he left unpaid the accounts of the refreshments called forth by the heat of his conversation". The pastime continued with renewed ardor, and ended up by supplanting politics.

22 LE BOEUF À LA MODE

6-8 rue de Valois

It was in the old Hôtel Mélusine, which still has its lovely balconies, that two brothers from Marseilles founded the restaurant *Boeuf à la mode* in 1792, a place where bouillabaisse and cod à la Provençale could be had. The establishment was to have a long life.

23 THE CHURCH OF SAINT-ROCH

It was on the staircase of this building that the fate of the Royalist insurrection of 13 Vendémiaire (October 5, 1795) was decided. Barras had asked Generals Bonaparte and Brune to help him defend the Convention threatened by the uprisings of the sections of Le Peletier and the Filles Saint Thomas, whose troops under the command of General Danican took their stand on the steps of the church, 200 meters from the Tuileries. At four that afternoon a piece of eight was set up in the cul-de-sac du Dauphin (Rue Sainte-Roch) and, loaded with grape, opened fire on Bonaparte's orders. At six o'clock it was all over. There were two hundred dead or wounded among the section men, and about the same number on the other side.

THE JACOBINS
Place du Marché Saint-Honoré

In 1613, the Dominicans settled here and the Parisians immediately dubbed them Jacobins, in imitation of their brothers in Rue Saint-Jacques. In Rue Saint-Honoré the monks had an area of ten French acres on which they built a chapel and convent buildings.

At the time of the Revolution, the convent housed sixty brothers and twenty novices, generally held to be conservative. Even so, in November 1789, they agreed to rent their library, for 200 francs a year, to the Société des Amis de la Constitution, heir to the *Club breton* founded in Versailles when the estates-general were opened. Thus for a few months, the monks still there lived side by side with the first members of the club known as "des Jacobins": Barnave, Mirabeau, Danton, Robespierre, Lameth, Sieyès, Condorcet, later Choderlos de Laclos. Apparently, however, the friars, to keep things separate, reserved for themselves the main entrance, while the members of the club came in through a secondary door... which still exists. It is the door at number 8 Rue Saint-Hyacinthe, through which we can see pass in our

▷ **Convent of the Jacobins.** All that remains in a former back entrance (Rue Saint-Hyacinthe).

△ **A Session of the Club of the Jacobins, in the Convent Library** (engraving, Musée Carnavalet). The religious decoration was still there.

◁ **Closing of the Club of the Jacobins on 10 Thermidor** (engraving, Musée Carnavalet). Shown is the chapel of the former convent where the club held its meetings at first in the library (in the attic) and afterwards in the chapel itself. On the right, tree of Liberty.

mind's eye the impeccable Robespierre, Danton, rather frowzy, or Dumas, future president of the revolutionary Tribune, in his outfit of fine red cloth. "A hundred living witnesses", Nodier was to write, "have not forgotten that that habit of blood was his gala habit".
From there, the members of the club reached the library, situated, it seems, in the attic of the chapel, lined with bookshelves and dominated by a fresco from which St. Thomas of Aquinas presided over the Revolutionary debates.
Some of the Dominicans did attend the sittings but in October 1790 the Assembly decided to suppress the convent, the friars left and the club remained the sole master where the members could now enter through the large doorway in Rue Saint-Honoré.
But the library had become too small for all these new members, one of whom was the future Louis-Philippe, and the Société decided to move into the chapel, where the first session took place on May 29, 1791. The history of the club, which it is not our task to relate, but which was determining up to 9 Thermidor, unfolded here. On July 28, 1794, the room was closed by Legendre, one of the members of the Convention, suddenly converted to the moderate wing, and the year after, the Convention decided to use the site of the convent, crossed by a street, for the construction of a market which took the name of 9 Thermidor. Things kept dragging out until Napoleon, vengefully pursuing the old Jacobins, had this symbolic structure demolished. The market, built by the architect Molinos and inaugurated in 1810, consisted of four covered markets and a fountain. Rebuilt in 1865, it was torn down in 1958 and replaced by an enormous structure in reinforced concrete which houses the offices of the police and the fire department. It is currently being debated whether to replace it with something esthetically more suitable.
But while the convent with the exception of the doorway we mentioned no longer exists, the surrounding district still looks as it did during the Revolution: the two sides of the Rue du Marché Saint-Honoré are old and also, with a few exceptions, the north and east sides of the square. These bourgeois houses, often bulging, often ornamented with charming balconies, witnessed the passage of the Jacobins, who began and continued discussions that were often unrealistic and exalted as the Revolution became more intransigent. Many of them may have frequented the cafe at the corner where the street meets the square, still to be seen with its original wrought ironwork, a rarity for Paris.

THE GUILLOTINE AND ITS FIRST ITINERARY
Rue Saint-Honoré

From May of 1793 to June of 1794, every day except the decade (10th day), what is now the first *arrondissement* was traversed in its entire length by the procession of tumbrils escorted by guards which, late in the afternoon, took the condemned prisoners to the guillotine in Place de la Révolution, now Place de la Concorde. This procession left the courtyard of the Palace of Justice, turned into the Rue de la Barillerie (Boulevard du Palais), the Pont au Change and began its journey up the length of the Rue Saint-Honoré, then the principle artery on the right bank, narrow and eternally packed with traffic. Many of the same houses still line the street and were witness to that daily caravan of death. One or the other of the prisoners cast a last glance at some of these facades, such as, for example, on the south between the Rue des Bordonnais and the Rue du Louvre, almost all the north side between the Rues des Bon Enfants and de Valois, du Marché Saint-Honoré and de la Sourdière, Vauvilliers and des Prouvaires. Many of these houses have retained their Louis XV or Louis XVI decor and were still almost new at the time: numbers 47, 111, 125, 320, 352 and 404. Many still have their wrought-iron railings, for example from 146 to 154, 350 and 352 to 370, and one must imagine, on those balconies, a crowd of spectators, vindicative, touched or simply curious to see the procession pass. From one of these privileged observatories, Danton and many of his friends watched Charlotte Corday take her last journey unto death, wearing the red gown of the parricide. The balcony at number 275, at the sign of the Holy Ghost, was particularly popular with devotees of these spectacles.

On October 26, 1793, a tumbril passed that, exceptionally, bore only one victim, the queen. After being sentenced she had asked to be led to her fate like Louis XVI, in a closed coach. Her request was refused but she was granted the mocking privilege of going alone in the tumbril.

▽ **Gobel, Bishop of Paris, Hébert and Chaumette Led to the Guillotine on March 14, 1794** (engraving by Berthault, Cabinet des Estampes). The procession passes in front of the portal of the club of the Jacobins in the Rue Saint-Honoré.

Dressed in a white petticoat and a chemise, her prematurely white hair cut off and hidden by a muslin bonnet compassionately provided for her by the concierge, her wrists bound behind her back, seated, with her bust erect as in Versailles four years before, her face impassive, she looked neither left nor right as she passed, sunk in one last meditation. From a window in the Rue Saint-Honoré, David, with a few swift strokes of his crayon, sketched an unforgettable portrait.

Upon her passage, the crowd on either side watched her go by in silence. But at the Croix du Trahoir, in front of Soufflot's fountain, which is still there, a gang of wretches launched a torrent of abuse at the defenseless bound woman on the tumbril, that fell on her like a pailful of dirty water. From then on, up to the scaffold, it was a flood of insults and obscenities.

Some of those condemned were already familiar with the Rue Saint-Honoré. When Philippe Egalité was taken from the Tribunal to the scaffold a crowd full of hate waited for him in front of his house, the Palais Royal. As insults filled the air he shrugged his shoulders and turned his head the other way. Lavoisier, taken to be executed on May 8, 1794, passed before the house with the sign of the iron cross (at present number 447) which belonged to him. On April 5, 1794, Bazire and Chabot were together in the same tumbril, behind that carrying Danton. Bazire was responsible for the law that suppressed the ecclesiastic habit and for the one which ordered the use of the familiar pronoun — *tu*. Chabot, an old Capuchin, was the inventor of the word sansculotte and had been the first to propose the suppression of the words *Sire* and *Votre Majesté*. The tumbril passed in front of their houses where they had been arrested shortly before: 77 for Bazire, 82 for Chabot.

The same day, Camille Desmoulins and Danton were also taken to the scaffold and shared the same tumbril. To the indifferent crowd, the former cried:

— It was I who called you to arms on July 14th! It was I who had you take up the national cockard! People, you are being duped! Those who uphold you, your best defendors, are being sacrificed!

— Take it easy, said Danton, and let this vile rabble be. But their passage before Robespierre's lodgings inspired his last apostrophe.

— Before long it will be your turn, Robespierre! Your house will be destroyed, he cried with that voice which had caused the crowds to tremble.

On his arrival in Place de la Concorde, the tribune sighted a tall emaciated figure in the crowd with whom he exchanged glances: it was the Abbot de Kerlevenan, a nonjuror priest who had blessed his second marriage and who, through half-closed lips, murmered an absolution. On 10 Thermidor there was another procession along the Rue Saint-Honoré. Two months had passed since Danton's prophecy. In honor of Robespierre and his friends — now called accomplices — the scaffold had been moved to the Place de la Révolution and those same crowds which but yesterday had acclaimed these dictators now thronged the streets to witness their downfall. They were a piteous batch: Robespierre, his jaws bound with a bloody bandage, was semi-conscious; his brother Augustin had a broken leg; Hanriot, one eye falling on his cheek, seemed a figure from a nightmare; the invalid Couthon, also wounded, was squeezed into the corner of one of the carts; alone, in the midst of the depressed med-

△ **Rue Saint-Honoré.** Many of the houses which still line the rue witnessed the tumbrils pass with their loads of prisoners.

ley, Saint-Just, still elegant, stood proud. The inhabitants of the Rue Saint-Honoré may well have asked themselves if the blood shed by those men had been for a just cause. We are still asking the same question.

25 ROBESPIERRE'S LODGINGS

398 rue Saint-Honoré

On July 17, 1791, after the insurrection in the Champ de Mars, Robespierre, who up till then had lived in the Rue de Saintonge, accepted the hospitality of Duplay, an old cabinetmaker. The house consisted of various buildings: on the side facing the street a doorway set next to a shop had a floor with four windows and attics above. Duplay's lodgings were at the back of the courtyard where a gabled main structure was connected to the building on the street by a two-story wing on the left. This was where Robespierre lived, with access from a staircase in the courtyard, which Duplay had had built for him. The Tribune, who paid a yearly rent of a thousand *livres*, had a closet and a bedroom with a bed in walnut, covered in blue damask with white flowers, once an old gown of the mistress of the house. Danton called the place "*le temple du rabot et du ragot*" (the temple of the plane and of gossip).

Augustin and Charlotte Robespierre, Maximilien's brother and sister, also lived for a while in the building on the street, as did Couthon. It was in this house that Elisabeth Duplay, the cabinetmaker's youngest daughter, fell in love with Philippe Lebas and a wedding ensued. In their house at the back of the courtyard, the Duplays

△ **Robespierre's house.** At the back, Duplay's dwelling, with extra storeys. The room occupied by the Incorruptible was on the first floor of the building on the left (window behind the glass canopy).

often received the circle of their great man's acquaintances: Desmoulins, Couthon, Saint-Just, David, Prudhon, Collot d'Herbois, La Revellière-Lepeaux.

Robespierre left the house the morning of 9 Thermidor never to return. When, the day after, he was led to the guillotine, a screaming mob obliged the procession to stop before the house, while they splattered the facade with the blood of an ox.

In the days that followed, the entire Duplay family was arrested. The cabinetmaker's wife was found strangled in her cell in Sainte-Pélagie.

The places can still be identified despite the changes that have taken place. The building on the street has been raised and the portal done away with. Duplay's house is now four stories higher. To the right of the courtyard, in place of the original garden, another wing has been built, opposite the building where Robespierre lodged and which has also been raised but where his bedroom and the closet still exist, as well as the small rooms next to them where a son and nephew of Duplay lived. That wing now houses a bar-restaurant, "Le Robespierre".

26 PLACE VENDÔME

The square still looks the way it did during the Revolution, except for the ornament in the center. An equestrian statue of Louis XIV by Girardon, outstanding both for its size and style and set here in 1699, was overthrown on October 12, 1792, a century after its fusion, and the pieces were sent to be melted down. Only the left foot was saved and is now in the Louvre. The square became "place des Piques".

The empty base was used by David when the body of Le Peletier de Saint-Fargeau was exhibited to the public in a magniloquent scenario after his funeral services. Later many projects were presented for a new central decoration but not until the Empire was the problem resolved with the erection of the Vendôme column.

Many manifestations took place here in Revolutionary times: the archives of the order of Saint-Esprit were burned, severed heads were exhibited, and in 1796 the incineration of the tables of the assignats took place.

The facade of the Ministry of Justice is still, except for the pediment decoration which was transformed more than once, the one which Danton saw when, the day after the 10th of August, he settled into the Ministry of Justice and to all effects became head of the government, with Desmoulins and Fabre d'Eglantine as collaborators. It was here in his office on the first floor that he did all he could to galvanize the French resistance, here he received the young Louis Philippe, showing him his responsibilities in the September massacres.

Lastly, on the ground floor, the facade of the Chancellery still has a souvenir of the Revolution: an incised meter, the story of which appears in that of the Rue de Vaugirard.

▽ **Facade of the Ministry of Justice**, Place Vendôme.

27 HÔTEL

1-3 rue d'Antin

This town house, built in 1720 and confiscated by the Revolution, was the town hall of *arrondissement* II from 1795 to 1833, and it was here that the marriage of Napoleon and Josephine de Beauharnais was celebrated on March 1796.

The ceremony had been set for eight in the evening and the document prepared had falsified their ages, making Josephine younger and Napoleon older than they really were. One of the witnesses was not yet of age and could therefore not figure as such. Bonaparte was two hours

△ **The Rue des Colonnes**, an interesting architectural ensemble built during the Revolution.

late and arrived like a gust of wind, saying:
— Monsieur mayor, marry us immediately.
The decoration of the room has been preserved.

28 RUE DES COLONNES

This may be the only monumental ensemble of the period still intact. During the ancien régime it was the site of the Hôtel de Chaspou de Verneuil, whose lands were turned into lots in 1792. An uncovered passageway between the Rue Feydeau and Rue des Filles Saint-Thomas was erected on this area, with specifications that imposed a uniformity on the buildings and covered galleries. The unknown architect thus conceived of arcades with Doric columns and palmette capitals.
Tradition narrates that when Bonaparte left the Theater Feydeau on the evening of October 4, 1795 (12 Vendémiaire, year IV), he encountered the Le Paletier division which was beating a retreat in this passageway (later to become a street) and went to offer his services to Barras.

29 MUSÉE GRÉVIN

10 boulevard Montmartre

The authentic bathtub in which Marat died appears in the scene depicting the death of the tribune.

30 HÔTEL D'AUGNY

6 rue Drouot

This town house, built in 1746-48 for d'Augny, remained the property of his heirs during the Revolution. They rented it out in 1794 and it became one of the numerous dance halls which flourished after Thermidor. The famous "balls of the Victims" were organized here, balls which only the close relations of those who had been decapitated could attend.

31 HÔTEL BOTTEREL-QUINTIN

44 rue des Petites Ecuries

The most important decorative ensemble from the days of the Revolution may well be that preserved here. The Count de Botterel-Quintin, who had bought the hôtel in 1785, added a dining room between 1790 and 1793. Eight meters long and five wide, with hemicycles at each end, the dome over it is decorated with a frieze depicting a bacchanale, attributed to Prudhon. Under the cornice there is a stucco decoration of cupids, sphinxes, semi-nude women. Between the columns, niches alternate with painted panels. The boudoir on the first floor, decorated in the same period, represents Pompeian motives, with cranes and Cupid riding a panther.

▽ **Hôtel Botterel-Quintin**. The dining room.

32 HÔTEL BOURRIENNE

58 rue d'Hauteville

This town house, begun in 1787, was finished in 1792 for the Lormier-Lagraves whose daughter Fortunée had just married the general supplier of the army Antoine Hamelin. The adventurous career of the lovely Mme Hamelin began here, where she lived until 1798. Her receptions were famous. The Victories which decorate the facade on the garden may date to that period, as does the Pompeian decoration in the bedroom, where the famous Merveilleuse received numerous guests.

33 THE SAINT-LAZARE PRISON

Area of the 107 rue de Faubourg Saint-Denis

The public garden known as Square Alban Satragne now stands on the site of the principal building of the Maison de Saint-Lazare, where Saint Vincent of Paola died in 1660. The congregation of the Mission Priests had an immense enclosure there, which occupied the area between what are now the Rue du Faubourg Saint-Denis, Rue du Faubourg Poissonnière, de Paradis and de Dunkerque. On July 13, 1789, the house was invaded and sacked by a band of two hundred malefactors on the pretext of looking for food. The congregation was suppressed in April 1792, and the silver reliquary of Saint Vincent of Paola sent to be melted, but the relics were left to the monks (they are at present in the chapel in 95 Rue de Sèvres). The following year, the ensemble of buildings was transformed into a prison, the prison Lazare. Between eight and nine hundred inmates were interned on four floors, each of which was traversed by three dark corridors, closed by gates, and smelling like a lair. André Chénier and Roucher, who went to the guillotine together on 7 Thermidor, were interned here, as was the famous Baron de Trenck, who had spent most of his life in prison, Mme de Montmorency-Laval, the last abbess of Montmartre, Admiral d'Estaing, all of whom were guillotined.

Others survived: Hubert Robert, who left many views of the prison, the dancer Mlle Dervieux, the Marquis de Sade and also Aimée de Coigny, the inspiration for André Chénier's elegy, "Jeune captive" and her lover Montrond: a hundred gold louis wisely distributed moved back the date of their execution, and they were saved.

34 HÔTEL PINSOT

4 rue Saint-Georges

This town house was built and decorated between May 8, 1792, when the land was acquired, and 4 Fructidor year XII (August 22, 1804), when Pinsot resold the hôtel. Its only outstanding feature on the street is a door with typical leaves, but the facade on the curved courtyard has retained its columns and a frieze of women and sphinxes. Inside one can still see the bathroom with friezes of tritons and mythological figures, a dining room with composite pilasters which frame panelled doors and decorated niches, an octagonal drawing room with a dome, and with bas reliefs in stucco with antique subjects, a bedroom with stucco overdoor decoration. It is the leading example in Paris of Directory architecture and decoration together.

35 RUE DE LA VICTORIE

Until 8 Nivôse year VI (December 28, 1797) this street was called Chantereine, in remembrance of the frogs which once had croaked in the swamps there. But when the municipality decided, without the hint of a smile, "that it was convenient to have all signs of royalty disappear", it was rebaptised Rue "de la Victoire", in honor of Napoleon, who lived there, at Josephine's house, on the site of numbers 58 and 60. It was here that he prepared the coup d'etat of 18 Brumaire.

Traces of the avenue which led to the house can still be detected at no. 60, with a tree which may date back to the 18th century.

36 HÔTEL LAKANAL

20 rue de la Chaussee d'Antin

In 1795, the Royalist advocate Jean-Baptiste Lakanal, brother of the famous member of the Convention, decided to have the architect Henry build him a hôtel in the Rue de Mont-Blanc, a fashionable district. Work began in 1796 and at that time Lakanal bought a whole series of curious remains of revolutionary vandalism.

The facade of Notre Dame de Paris, after the 13th century, was decorated above the portals by a gallery of figures representing the kings of Judah, the legendary ancestors of Christ which, in the eyes of the people of Paris, represented the first kings of France. After the fall of the monarchy, on order of the Commune of Paris, the entrepreneur Varin, between December 1793 and September 1794, decapitated and tore down the statues and deprived the cathedral of much of its sculptural decoration. The fragments were piled up at the foot of the monument until June, 1796, when they were put up for sale. Lakanal bought them, using the shapeless blocks, broken up into rubble, in the foundations of his hôtel, while he had a ditch dug outside the building where the fragments of sculpture and architecture were carefully placed, out of religious and monarchic piety, perhaps in hope of better days.

But he died in 1800 and it was not until 1977 in the course of works that the 364 fragments, consisting of sculpture from the portals of the cathedral and twenty-one heads from the gallery of Kings, were discovered. They are now in the museum of Cluny.

The town house was composed of two communicating constructions on either side of a tree-lined avenue which led to the house itself. This arrangement was modified later when additional structures sprang up and floors were added. But we still have the central portal on the street, framed by Doric columns, with its Ionic porch.

The hôtel was bought on February 25, 1799 by General Moreau, who held many meetings there in preparation for his coup d'etat of 18 Brumaire.

▷ **Head of one of the Statues in the Gallery of the Kings on Notre-Dame, pulled down during the Revolution** (Musée de Cluny).

THE CHAPELLE EXPIATOIRE
Square Louis XVI

In 1721, the new cemetery of the parish of the Madeleine was installed here in an area that was prevalently swampy. Since the Tuileries formed part of this parish, the numerous Swiss Guards massacred when the palace was taken on August 10th were buried here, as well as the prisoners guillotined in the Place de la Concorde between August 26, 1792 and March 24, 1794. Among these, Louis XVI (January 21, 1793), Charlotte Corday (July 13), Marie Antoinette (October 15), the Girondins (October 31), Philippe Egalité (November 7), Mme Roland (November 9), Mme du Barry (December 8). All in all almost three thousand corpses. The body of the king, dressed in grey trousers and a jacket of white piquet, had been placed, his head between his legs, in an open coffin that was loaded onto a cart. This then headed up the Rue de la Bonne-Morue (Boissy d'Anglas) of which some of the houses (no. 6, 8, 18) are still those that watched the procession pass, then the Faubourg Saint-Honoré and the Rue d'Anjou. The body was let down into a pit dug three meters from the wall that ran along the Rue d'Anjou. Marie Antoinette also had the right to a special ditch, paying the grave diggers twenty-five *livres*.

After 1794, the cemetery was closed and sold first to a carpenter, and then in 1802 to a neighbor, Pierre-Louis Desclozeaux, who had at the time made note of the places where the king and queen were buried. He kept the cemetery in good condition and sold it in 1814 to Louis XVIII, who had excavations carried out. The presumed bones of Louis XVI and of Marie Antoinette were transferred to Saint-Denis, and between 1816 and 1826 Fontaine and Lebas built a monument known as the Chapelle Expiatoire on the site of the cemetery. In the small cloister, a sort of graveyard which induces meditation, the arcades house funerary monuments to the memory of the Swiss troops of August 10th, to Charlotte Corday, and also to Philippe Egalité, who has thus been pardoned by his family. In the chapel, two sculptures by Bosio and Corbot depict Louis XVI and Marie Antoinette, and the altar in the crypt is on the site of the king's grave.

The question has been raised as to whether these are really the remains of the royal couple. Chateaubriand declared that he had recognized Marie Antoinette by her smile, a statement both grotesque and inopportune: actually fragments of the stockings the queen wore at the Conciergerie were found. For Louis XVI, the presence of a deep ditch, with layers of lime, seems to dispel all doubts. If it be added that the grandson of one of the grave-diggers of 1793 confirmed the localization indicated by Desclozeaux, this cross-identification seems more than likely, repudiating the affirmation of Barras, a gratuitous hoaxer, that the man who rests in Saint-Denis in the tomb of the king was actually "general" Hanriot, one of the most sinister figures of the Revolution, and who is probably not buried in this cemetery.

▷ **The Chapelle Expiatoire:** Louis XVI supported by an angel, by Bosio.

▽ **The Chapelle Expiatoire**.

PLACE DE LA RÉVOLUTION
Place de la Concorde

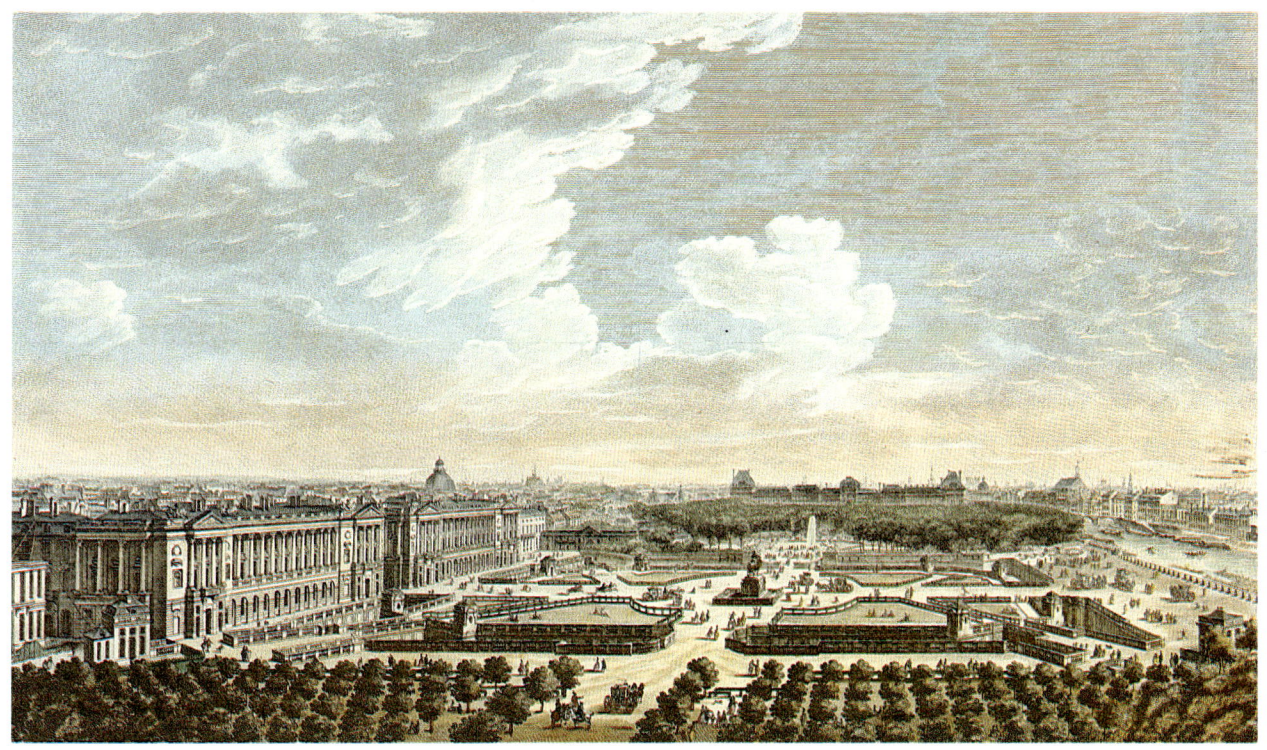

△ **Perspective View of the Place Louis XV before the Revolution** (engraving, Musée Carnavalet).

The view over the square from the terrace of the Jeu de Paume is still much like what a passerby might have seen in the days of the Directory. After 1770 the palace by Gabriel stood on the right, various moats were situated below the balustrades that can still be seen, and one could go down through Gabriel's sentry boxes which are now topped by statues. The square, then as now, was joined to the left bank by the Pont Louis XVI, built by Perronet between 1787 and 1791 and finished with stones from the Bastille. Finally, it was said, "they will be trodden by the feet of the people".

It quickly became one of the most important sites in the history of the Revolution. On July 12, 1789, the square was invaded by a gang of rioters carrying the busts of Necker and the Duc d'Orléans. The Prince de Lambesc, at the head of a detachment of Royal-Allemand, dispersed them at the entrance to the Tuileries, but the event did more for the cause of the Revolution than for that of the royal government. The following day, the rioters invaded the Magazin in their search for arms with which to attack the Bastille. All they found, and carried off, were a few parade arms: the spear of Marshal de Boucicaut, Du Guesclin's saber, Francis I's sword, and two silver cannons given to Louis XIV by the king of Siam.

After the fall of the Bastille, the king returned to Paris on July 17th. The authorities and numerous members of the Assembly received him on the quay and the Gardes Françaises were lined up in the square while the crowd of bystanders cried: *Vive la Nation*! *Vive le Roi*!"

On October 6th, brought back from Versailles, the royal family crossed here on their way to the Tuileries. It was the scene for one manifestation after the other. On August 10, 1792, the last Swiss Guards withdrew from the Tuileries. They were received with gunfire by the National Guard and, the day after, the statue of Louis XV by Bouchardon, erected in 1763, was pulled down. The right hand of the statue is still to be seen in the Louvre. Place Louis XV then became Place de la Révolution.

From September 11th to 16th, 1792, the Magazin was the scene for the theft of the crown jewels, perpetrated with extraordinary ease, and it was to punish the thieves that, for the first time, the guillotine was raised on the square the following October 13th.

For the execution of Louis XVI (January 21, 1793) it was placed about twelve meters from the pedestal of the statue of Louis XV in the direction of the Champs-Elysées, in other words at a spot that is now approximately between the obelisk and the statue of Brest.

The king, after mounting the scaffold, attempted to address the crowd that thronged the square behind the troops, but his voice was covered by the roll of drums. Who had given the order? For a long time "general" Santerre boasted of the fact, and despite all doubts later expressed it seems to be the truth, in line with the accounts of eye-witnesses who also confirmed the great dignity the king displayed at this moment.

On August 10, 1793, for the anniversary of the fall of the

monarchy, a bronzed plaster statue of Liberty by the sculptor Lemot was inaugurated. A spear in one hand, the Phrygian cap on her head, she was set up on the old pedestal. But the cubic shape of the latter was not suited to a seated statue which, in a comment of the times, looked at the Tuileries "askance and with an evil eye". At her feet, the royal insignia were solemnly burned.
The guillotine had returned here on May 11th, erected permanently between the statue of Liberty and the entrance to the Tuileries. It stayed there thirteen months, during which time Charlotte Corday was executed (a headsman's assistant slapped her head as he held it aloft), as well as Marie Antoinette, the Girondins, Philippe Egalité, Mme Roland, who addressed the statue with the famous words:

◁ **The Place de la Concorde as it is today**. The obelisk stands on the site of the statue of Liberty. The scaffold was set up on the right.

◁ **Place Louis XV before the Revolution, Seen from the Tuileries** (French school, 18th cent., Musée Carnavalet). In the foreground, sculptoral groups by Coysevox framing the entrance to the Tuileries. In the background, the monument to Louis XV by Bouchardon and Pigalle.

◁ **Charge of Lambesc's Dragoons at the Tuileries on July 12, 1789** (J. B. Lallemand, Musée Carnavalet). In the background, the Place Louis XV, with the monument to the king.

▽ **Plundering the Garde Meuble for Arms on July 14, 1789** (Prieur, drawing, Musée Carnavalet).

Following pages:
Destruction of the Emblems of the Monarchy on August 10, 1793 (P. A. Demachy, Musée Carnavalet). On the left, Lemot's statue of Liberty, set on the base where the statue of Louis XV formerly stood.

△ **An Execution in the Place de la Révolution in 1793-94** (P. A. Demachy, Musée Carnavalet).

▷ **Fête de la Fédération, in the Champ de Mars, on July 14, 1790** (P. A. Demachy, Musée Carnavalet). On the right, in front of the Military School, the tribune for the king and the authorities.

▽ **The Concorde as it is today, view of the Tuileries**. A small garden for the Dauphin was installed in the moat bordering the terrace. In the back right, the present Ministry of the Admiralty shields the royal Garde Meuble which was broken into in September 1792.

— Liberty, Liberty, how many crimes are committed in your name!
And others still — Mme du Barry, gasping and sighing, Hébert, Chaumette, Malesherbes, Lavoisier, Mme Elisabeth, Danton, who said to the executioner:
— You will show my head to the people. It's well worth it!
All in all, a thousand one hundred victims in thirteen months.
But the Parisians were tired of that spectacle, and the scaffold was transferred on June 9, 1794 to the Bastille, then to Place du Trône renversé. It returned here after 9 Thermidor for the execution of Robespierre and his friends and once more in May 1795, for that of the insurrectionists of 1 Prairial.
On 5 Floréal year II (April 24, 1794) the Convention also deliberated to embellish the square by moving the horses made by Cousteau for the fountain of Marly to the Place de la Révolution. In July-August 1795 the operation was directed by the architect Lannoy who designed the pedestals and widened the Champs-Elysées, flanked ever since by two broad sidewalks, to show the steeds off to their best advantage: the layout of one of the finest views in Paris is thanks to the Revolution.
Finally, during one of its last sessions (4 Brumaire year IV) the Convention decreed that the square be named Place de la Concorde: the famous name of one of the most illustrious plazas in the world dates from this time.

THE FAUBOURG SAINT-GERMAIN

CHAMP DE MARS

39

Even though the Champ de Mars, now much smaller than it was during the Revolution, has changed completely, the most important events that took place there can still be evoked.

For the anniversary of the taking of the Bastille on July 14, 1790, the Fête de la Fédération was held here. The culminating moment was a mass celebrated on an altar raised in the midst of the terrain which, in the preceding weeks, had been transformed into a small valley flanked by two terraced escarpments. Thousands of volunteers from all social classes had helped, working side by side. It is said that a judge, a dancer from the Opera, a Benedictine nun, a soldier were seen all pulling the same wagon, an outstanding coincidence for a period with a taste for allegory.

Talleyrand, bishop of Autun, officiated, in front of two hundred priests dressed in white tunics barred with the tricolor, assisted by the Abbot Louis, future minister of the Restoration, to whom he whispered:

— Above all, don't make me laugh!

After this, the oath of allegiance to the Nation was taken, first by La Fayette, and then by three hundred thousand spectators. The king, seated in a tribune in front of the military school, also swore allegiance, as did the royal family. The enthusiasm of the spectators was dampened by a torrential rain.

After the king had returned from Varennes, on July 17, 1791, demonstrators under the auspices of the club of the Cordeliers attempted to have a petition asking for the dethronement of the king signed on the "Altar of the Country". La Fayette, commander of the National Guard, and Bailly, mayor of Paris, decided to disperse them. The red banner, symbol of martial law, was unfurled and the square cleared: there were about fifty dead.

To punish Bailly for the role he had played in those circumstances, sixteen months later when he was sentenced to death the guillotine was raised in the center of the garden, on the former-site of the altar of the Fête de la Fédération. As the condemned prisoner was standing at the foot of the scaffold, some of those present declared they did not want to see the earth of the Champ de Mars sullied with the blood of such a criminal and demanded that the guillotine be moved to one of the moats flanking the garden. In the meanwhile Bailly impassively waited and was subjected to a barrage of mud and spit. Observing that he was shivering, one of the headsman's helpers asked him — Are you trembling?

— Yes, citizen, but it is because of the cold.

Finally his head fell at the corner of the embankment and what is now Avenue de la Bourdonnais.

The Fête of the Supreme Being, begun at the Tuileries,

ended at the Champ de Mars on June 8, 1974. "The sections in alphabetic order, three military bands, a wagon of Liberty pulled by eight oxen, the deputies with bouquets. As president, Robespierre, in a blue dress-coat, preceded his colleagues. The retinue went around a symbolic mountain along steep paths, in the midst of tombs, a pyramid and a Greek temple. "Père de l'Univers..." was sung. At the last line, a cannon was fired, all embraced and then went their way while the Convention as a single unit reached the hall of their session" (Tulard). In September 1798, the Directory organized an industrial fair here, ancestor to all the universal expositions to be held thereafter. It was enclosed by a square fence and surrounded by a portico of sixty-eight arcades. The prizes were assigned to the Maison Bréguet for clock-making, Firmin-Didot for printing, Conté for his crayons, Erard for his pianos.

40 AUBERGE DU SOLEIL D'OR

226 rue de Vaugirard

This old inn, which has kept its sign (a golden sun), was where the monarchic conspirators met in 1791, and under the guidance of a citizen from Vaugirard, Thévenot, planned the "plot of the Golden Sun" to exterminate the Jacobins and consolidate the position of Louis XVI on the throne. One of the conspirators denounced Thévenot, who was arrested. In 1796, another conspiracy, known as "camp de Grenelle", to overthrow the Directory, fomented by partisans of Babeuf, took place here. Manipulated by police instigators, and denounced, they were arrested the night of 8-9 September (23-24 Fructidor). Thirty-one of the one hundred and thirty-two conspirators arrested went before the firing squad.

△ **Fête of the Supreme Being in Champ de Mars on 20 Prairial year II** (P. A. Demachy, Musée Carnavalet). Note the decorations prepared for the event: colonnade, statue, allegorical column, mound with the tree of Liberty.

▽ **The Champ de Mars as it is today.** The central basin is approximately on the site of the altar of the Fête de la Fédération.

41 HÔTEL

83 rue du Cherche-Midi

In 1789 this town house belonged to Count Stanislas de Clermont-Tonnerre, an aristocrat of liberal ideas. Deputy of the Nobility at the estates-general, he voted for the abolition of the privileges and pronounced himself in favor of the constitutional monarchy. Arrested after the flight of the king, then released, he was massacred on the threshold of his hôtel by a crowd instigated by one of his old servants on August 10, 1792. Thereafter, the house was occupied by the doctor, Cavanis, friend of Mirabeau, who died in his presence, and by Condorcet.

42 HÔPITAL LAËNNEC

42 rue de Sèvres

On April 12, 1796, the widow of the shoemaker Simon was admitted to this institution, once a hospice for incurables. Until the end of her life, twenty-three years later, she maintained that she had had a part in the escape of the Dauphin Louis XVII.

43 OLD CONVENT OF THE RECOLLETS

85 rue du Bac

Before the Revolution the convent of the Recollets, which was installed here in 1637, stretched along the entire Rue du Bac, between the Rue de Grenelle and the Rue de Varenne. The church was built between 1693 and 1703. Closed in 1790, the convent was sold in 1797 and the church was transformed into a playhouse, the *Théâtre des Victoires Nationales*. It changed hands frequently and was transformed, but the building has preserved its pediment.

▽ **The chapel of the convent of the Récollets** was transformed into a theater during the Revolution.

△ The Hôtel de Galliffet as it is today.

44 HÔTEL DE GALLIFFET

73 rue de Grenelle

Simon de Galliffet had this town house rebuilt in the closing years of the realm and it was terminated when he had to emigrate in 1791. In 1794 the Committee of Public Safety allotted the "Maison Galliffet" to the Ministry of Foreign Affairs. The actual scope of the committee was that of reanimating Faubourg Saint-Germain, which emigration and sequesters had left deserted, and also to make the most of the fine houses the State had confiscated.

Various transformations were carried out inside, and the first minister to occupy the palace was Philibert Buchot, an incompetent who passed his days at the cafe playing billiards, followed by Charles Delacroix, the father of the painter, and lastly in July 1797, by Talleyrand who thus began a new career. The following December 6th he received Napoleon here in his office overlooking the garden, and on January 3rd, gave a great fête in the hôtel to celebrate the peace of Campo Formio: the enchanting decorations designed by Belanger left the five hundred guests speechless.

It was during this same party that Mme de Staël tried to catch Napoleon's attention and was snubbed. She never forgave him.

45 HÔTEL DE CHANALEILLES

12 rue de Chanaleilles

During the Revolution this old country house, built around 1770, became the property of Barras, who sold it in February 1799 to Mme Tallien, at the time the mistress of the banker Ouvrard, who seems to have financed the

△ **The Hôtel de Castries Being Pillaged on November 13, 1792** (engraving, by Berthault, Cabinet des Estampes).

purchase. She gave many a fête here. Originally a long boulevard which began in Rue de Babylone led to the house which was also surrounded by a large garden that disappeared with the opening of the Rue de Chanaleilles and Rue Bartet de Jouy.

and they were about to set fire to the building when La Fayette and the National Guard arrived. From his exile, the old marshal wrote: "It is impossible to see one's house pillaged, the house where one was born and which has been so lovingly embellished, without anguish. . .". After so many vicissitudes, the building became the Ministry of War in 1795. News of Napoleon's victories in Italy arrived here.

46 HÔTEL DE CASTRIES
72 rue de Varenne

Built at the beginning of the 18th century under Louis XVI, this town house belonged to the Marquis de Castries, marshal of France, who lived there with his son Armand-Charles. The latter, elected by the Nobility to the estates-general, was an ardent defender of royal privileges and soon found himself involved in a violent discussion with Lameth, who challenged him to a duel on November 12th. The encounter took place a few hours later: "I drove my sword", Castries was to write, "three or four inches into the lower part. The blow hit a tendon and he found himself in bad shape. . .".
The news spread rapidly through Paris that the sword was poisoned and a mob of rioters went to the hôtel de Castries. The young man managed to flee, but the house was invaded and all it contained was stolen or broken to bits. A print by Prieur shows the rabble throwing furniture and books from the window. Nothing was spared,

47 HÔTEL DE VILLARS
116 rue de Grenelle

During the Revolution, the hôtel, built in the middle of the 17th century and which at present houses the town hall of the VII *arrondissement*, belonged to the Duc de Brissac, commander of the Cents-Suisses. His mistress, Mme du Barry, had an apartment here and this was also where on the 6th of January 1791, after a sumptuous dinner, she learned of the theft of her box of jewels from her château of Louveciennes, a prelude to her arrest and execution three years later.
After the death of the duke in the massacre of Versailles on September 9, 1792, his daughter, the Duchess of Mortemart, inherited the hôtel, but it was requisitioned and entrusted to the custody of citizen Madiot, who complained of the damage caused to the rare plants in the garden by cows which had been pastured there.
In 1795 the building became the seat of the Ministry of the Interior.

48 HÔTEL CHANAC DE POMPADOUR
142 rue de Grenelle

Built around 1750 this town house was bought in 1785 by the Baron Pierre Victor de Besenval, commander of the Swiss Guards, who enlarged it and had the decoration finished. He was arrested in 1789 and, despite the calumnious pamphlets which were being circulated, was freed and returned home. Between January and June of 1790 Brongniart conceived the decoration in the dining room.

49 PALAIS BOURBON

The prince of Condé, owner of the Palais Bourbon, had emigrated three days after the fall of the Bastille and, in April 1792, the palace was confiscated, together with the neighboring Hôtel de Lassay. It was of course initially used as a prison, and after the 10th of August received about two hundred Swiss who had escaped the massacre. Then in 1795, the Hôtel de Lassay was turned over to one of the most outstanding institutions created by the Revolution, the Ecole Polytechnique. The following September, the palace itself was assigned to one of the two assemblies created by the Directory, the Council of Five Hundred. A room was needed for the sessions, which was not ready until January 21, 1798, exactly five years after the death of Louis XVI. For two years, discussions were held here, with one coup d'etat after the other alternately excluding the left or the right wing of the Assembly, until the day of 18 Brumaire when the Five Hundred were transferred to Saint-Cloud.

Only the decoration of this room, replaced during the Restoration, remains: six statues works by Lemot, Ramey, Masson, which in 1798 were set on either side of the tribune and are still preserved in Palais Bourbon; the president's armchair, and above all the famous tribune decorated with a relief by Lemot depicting Fame dictating to History. For about two centuries, the deputies have been deliberating in the midst of a Revolutionary decor.

50 HÔTEL DE SEIGNELAY
Ministère du Commerce, 80 rue de Lille

This building was sold in 1780 to the Duke of Béthune-Charost, who went to live there with his family, including his mother-in-law Mme de Tourzel, last governess of the *enfants* of France, who had the apartment to the left on the first floor. At the beginning of the Revolution, the duke, a very liberal soul, made a voluntary gift of most of his silver to the Mint. Arrested during the Terror, he was freed after six months. After 9 Thermidor, Mme de Tourzel and her daughter went every day to visit Mme Royal who was imprisoned at the Temple. She gave them many souvenirs and entrusted them with her dog, whose tomb is still in the garden of the house.

51 HÔTEL DE SALM
64 rue de Lille

In 1782, Frédéric III, prince of Salm-Kyrbourg, had the town house which carries his name built by Pierre Rousseau. It was finished in 1788, greatly upsetting the state of the prince's finances. At the beginning of the Revolution, Frédéric at first embraced the cause of the monarchy, but he soon adhered to the new ideas and joined the Duke of Orléans. In November 1789, La Fayette nominated him commander of a battalion of the National Guard, section of la Fontaine de Grenelle. He forwent his royal pension of twenty thousand *livres* even though his finances were in a disastrous state. On March 18, 1790, his furniture and personal belongings were seized and seals were affixed. He was once more condemned in January 1791. He then tried to get rid of his house and offered it in a lottery but without luck.

At the end of 1792, he abolished the feudal rights in his estates and introduced the French constitution. Then came the Terror and he thought it best to emigrate and leave for England with his young son and his sister, the Princess Amélie de Hohenzollern. At this point Josephine de Beauharnais asked him to take along her children, Hortense and Eugene. But their father was of another opinion: he had them stopped at Saint-Paul in Artois, and insisted they be returned to him.

This return was fatal to the prince who, on January 17, 1794, was arrested, a case of mistaken identity with his cousin, the Prince of Salm-Salm. The hôtel was perquisitioned and the Committee of Sûreté générale, despite the fact that they admitted their error, decided to keep the prince prisoner in his own house.

Two months later, denounced for a few imprudent words, Frédéric III was taken to the Carmes and thence to the guillotine, but Amélie continued to live here and Hortense and Eugene often came to see her.

The town house, temporarily confiscated, was then returned to the children of the prince, but it was heavily damaged by the explosion of the powderhouse of Grenelle on August 31, 1794 and all it contained was sold at public auction between December 1795 and April 1796. During this period it was occupied by an adventurer, Leuthereau, known as the Marquis of Beauregard, who received his mistress Mlle Lange, actress of the Théâtre français, here. On June 4, 1797, a club with progressive ideas, one of whose founders was Benjamin Constant, saw the light in one part of the building. The club was to be called the "club de Salm".

▽ **The Hôtel de Seignelay as it is today**.

△ Former portal of the Theatine convent.

52 HÔTEL DE ROQUELAURE

246 boulevard Saint-Germain

This town house, transformed by Lassurance for the Duchess de Roquelaure in 1722, belonged, after 1740, to Mathieu-François Molé, lord of Champlâtreux, who embellished it considerably.

On July 14, 1789, his grandson Mathieu, future prime minister of Louis Philippe, was in the doorway when a mob arrived threatening to set fire to the building. The family left the house, except for the old Mathieu-François, who had made up his mind to stand up to the mob. The house was saved. In November 1790 they were ordered to chisel off the "monarchic" motives from the carriage gateway.

On August 10, 1792, Edouard-François, son of Mathieu-François, was arrested, then released and carried back home in triumph. A few months later, he was once more arrested together with his wife, and imprisoned at the Jacobins of Rue Saint-Dominique (at present Direction de l'Artillerie, Place Saint-Thomas d'Aquin). They were soon released but, when the protest made by the members of Parliament against its suppression, a protest to which the president Mathieu-François Molé, who died in 1793, had subscribed, was discovered among the papers of the president de Rosambo, his son was arrested for the third time. Condemned on April 20, 1794, he was guillotined the same day. The hôtel was confiscated and turned over to the Commission of Agriculture and Arts.

53 OLD ENTRANCE TO THE CONVENT OF THE THEATINES

26 rue de Lille

The order of the Theatines owned a convent between the Quai Voltaire and Rue de Lille, with a lovely church built by Guarini. It was closed in 1790, the Theatines were expelled in April 1791, and their works of art deposited in the Musée des Monuments Français. In 1794 the church was transformed into a granary and sold in 1797 as property of the State. It was then torn down in 1821, but the portal of one of the entrances, built by Desmaisons in 1754, still remains. The pediment represents an angel originally holding a cross which was eliminated during the Revolution.

54 THE MUSÉE DES MONUMENTS FRANÇAIS

14 rue Bonaparte

The convent of the Petits Augustins was founded in 1608 by Queen Margot and terminated under the regency of Anne of Austria. All that still remains today is the first chapel, known as Chapelle des Louanges, covered with a dome, the second chapel, built next to it later, and the cloister, now known as courtyard of Mûrier (the Moor). That these buildings were preserved is thanks to Alexandre Lenoir, who, in 1791, succeeded in having the convent assigned to him as a warehouse for the works of art he did all he could to rescue from the revolutionary vandals, at times endangering his own life.

In 1795 this warehouse became the Musée des Monuments Français. Lenoir thus created a picturesque evocative collection in the buildings and, after 1797, in the garden, a collection that was to play an important role in the rebirth of the appreciation of history and an interest in the works of the past. It was one of the great creations of the Revolutionary period.

Under the Restoration, the museum was suddenly brutally suppressed. The buildings, transformed under Louis-Philippe into a School of Fine Arts, still clearly reveal Lenoir's installations, as in the central avant-corp of the château of Anet superposed on the facade of the chapel; the sculpture fragments arranged under the blind arcades of the second court. A part of the garden contains what remains of the Louvre and the Hôtel Legendre and a lesser known room, the chapel sacristy, with its remains of Parisian churches, still gives us an idea of this pre-Romanic museum complex.

▽ **Garden of the Ecole des Beaux-Arts**. It still looks somewhat as it did when it was the garden of the Musée des Monuments Français.

△ **A Room in the Musée des Monuments Français, in the Convent of the Petits-Augustins** (Hubert Robert, Musée du Louvre).

▷ **The Garden of the Musée des Monuments Français** (Hubert Robert, Musée Carnavalet).

55 MAISON DE BUZOT

3 quai Malaquais

The Convention had decided to raze the house and replace it with the inscription "*là fut la maison du roi Buzot*", but the events of Thermidor saved the building.

55 HÔTEL DE CHATEAUNEUF

5 quai Malaquais

At the beginning of the Revolution the Baroness de Korff lived on the second floor of this town house. Late in 1790 when preparing the flight of the royal family Ferson confided in her and she ordered the coach, paying 296,000 *livres*. When they left on June 20, 1791, Mme de Tourzel had a passport in the name of Mme de Korff.

56 CHAPELLE DE LA CHARITÉ

49 rue des Saints Pères

The Convention had decided to increase the number of hospitals and create schools of medicine. The doctor Corvisart and the architect Clavareau proposed installing the first of these schools in the old chapel of the hôpital de la Charité, built in the 18th century. Work was authorized in February 1795.

Clavareau separated the nave from the choir, which was transformed into an amphitheater, decorated with a palmette cornice. This amphitheater, famous in the history of medicine for the lectures held there by Corvisart, and later by Laënnec, still exists.

In the lower part of the nave, the architect built a large atrium decorated with sixteen Ionic columns, greatly admired by his contemporaries, and which is at present the orthodox church of Saint Wladimir le Grand.

The facade is still marked by the modifications Clavareau carried out, in particular the door surmounted by a high relief depicting Aesculapius and framed by two fine lictoreal fasces, one of the rare signs the Revolution left on the Paris landscape.

△ **The church of Saint-Germain des Prés as it is today.** Plundered during the Revolution, the two bell towers framing the choir had to be torn down.

▽ **The former Chapel of the Charité.** It has retained traces of the transformations it was subjected to during the Revolution.

57 ST. GERMAIN DES PRES

The Church

The abbey Saint-Germain des Prés was suppressed in 1790. In February 1791 it became a parish church and a year later was closed. In February 1794 a refinery for saltpetre was installed here which functioned for eight years. The salpetrous waters which ran down the walls and piers and filtered down into the foundations damaged the building so heavily that in 1801 there was talk of tearing it down.

The Refectory

After the suppression of the abbey, the splendid refectory built by Pierre de Montereau served as a powder deposit from 1793 on. The deposit exploded at 9 o'clock in the evening on August 19, 1794. The refectory collapsed and the library, on the floor above, was devastated by a fire which was not subdued until two in the morning. Many manuscripts however were saved, in particular Pascal's *Pensées*. This was the end of the refectory whose western gable can still be seen in the stairwell of number 16, Rue de l'Abbaye.

The Abbey Prison

The building which stood on the site across from numbers 135-137 of what is now the Boulevard Saint-Germain, was a sort of cube, flanked by corner towers and was built by Gamard in the 17th century. Entrance was through a low narrow doorway (on an axis with the present boulevard) in the massive facade, "a hole in the wall", said an inmate.

The prison soon made the news. On June 30, 1789, a procession of demonstrators arrived to free eleven French guards who had refused to load their arms. On February 28, 1791, the members of the "dagger conspiracy" were shut up here. The day after August 10th, it received thirty-two Swiss and twenty-six guards who had escaped the massacre of the Tuileries. They were joined by relatives of the *émigrés*, aristocrats, the count of Montmorin, former minister of Foreign Affairs, the marquis of Sombreuil, governor of the Invalides, and also Beaumarchais, who succeeded in being relased after four days.

On Sunday morning, September 2, 1792, the news spread contemporaneously throughout Paris of the fall of Verdun and of the discovery of a so-called conspiracy "on the part of the aristocrats and the non-juror priests aided by highwaymen and villains to assassinate all the good citizens shut up in the prisons". Some fiacres transporting sixteeen prisoners to the Abbey were stopped at the Buci crossroads. The throats of four were cut then and there and another nine were massacred when they arrived at the prison.

The assassins then went to the Carmes, later returning to the Abbey where they set up two improvised "tribunals" in the prison chancellery and on the first floor of the hospice (area of what is now Square Laurent Prache): one of them was presided by the porter Maillard, nicknamed "*tapedur*". ("rough pat").

Of the 357 prisoners who appeared before the "court", 307 were massacred, some in front of the prison doorway in the Rue Sainte-Marguerite (now Rue Gozlin), most of them in the "large garden courtyards" (corner of Rue Bonaparte and Rue de l'Abbaye). Billaud-Varenne made an official appearance during the massacre, congratulated the assassins, and promised them wages.

The old houses of Rue Gozlin, Rue de la Petit Boucherie and Rue de l'Echaudé witnessed this spectacle: the corpses were displayed everywhere, within and without the Abbey, and those who came to take in the sight complained they could see nothing at night. The committee of the section then had twenty-four lamps set near the bodies. The Abbey massacres were particularly grim for they were turned into a spectacle fostered by the word and ac-

▽ **Massacres in Front of the Prison of the Abbey in September 1792** (engraving by Berthault, Musée Carnavalet).

tion of dozens of spectators drawn by curiosity, hate, sadism. Above all women.

For a while the prison remained almost empty. The first prisoner of particular importance was Mme Roland, in June of 1793. "I entered those filthy four walls, at the center of which was a cot without covers, and glimpsed a window with double bars. I was struck by that odor which a person used to a meticulously clean dwelling finds in those that are not. I realized that it was really a prison in which one had to live".

Other inmates included Brissot, Charlotte Corday, Choderlos de Laclos who saw Philippe Egalité here for the last time. Some left for the guillotine. Those who remained were freed on 9 Thermidor.

58 HOUSE
6 rue Grégoire de Tours

Seventeenth-century sculptured sign depicting a wild man, holding a club. During the Revolution it was called "le sansculotte".

△ Café Procope as it is now.

▽ **Sign in the Rue Grégoire de Tours**. It was baptised at the time «le sans-culotte».

▷ **The Cour du Commerce** has changed but little since the Revolution. On the left, Marat's typography, above which Brissot's widow later opened a reading room. Across from it, the restaurant «la Guillotine» stands on the site of the workshop where this device was designed.

well as during the Revolution it was regularly frequented by the celebrities of the moment who lived in the neighbourhood: Danton, Desmoulins, Brune, Marat, Legendre, Fabre d'Eglantine, as well as numerous "Cordeliers". It has been asserted, and is in all likelihood true, that the orders for the attacks on the Tuileries of June 20 and August 10, 1792, were emanated from here, and perhaps those for the September massacres as well. Here, too, it is said, a certain citizen Julian appeared one day in 1789 with "*le bonnet phrygien qui coiffait Pâris*" (the Phrygian bonnet Paris, i.e. the mythical hero, wears), which betrays, as often during the Revolution, a rather superficial... knowledge of history. This was the beginning of this fashion (one of these bonnets is exhibited in a showcase on the ground floor).

The room on the left, with its portraits of famous customers, provides us with a good idea of what it was like at the time. The first floor is decorated with wallpaper that reproduces the original papering in the hall of the Committee of Public Safety in the Tuileries, and the table at which Voltaire used to sit can still be seen. It served as votive altar for the passage of the mortal remains of Voltaire himself, and of Le Peletier de Saint-Fargeau and of Marat, on their way to the Panthéon.

59 CAFÉ PROCOPE
13 rue de l'Ancienne Comédie

In 1675 Francesco Procopio dei Coltelli from Palermo had opened a cafe here which benefitted by the fact that the Comédie-française was installed across the way in 1689. Extremely popular at the end of the 18th century as

59 HÔTEL
16 rue de l'Ancienne Comédie

When he came back from England, Marat occupied a three-room apartment in this town house built in 1750, and in November of 1789 he set up his typography in the cellar, financed by his companion Simone Evrard. It was here on January 22, 1790, that they came to arrest him for "*libelles et propos incendiaires et séditieux*", but he had already fled.

▷ **10 Rue de la Huchette**. The staircase is still the one used by General Bonaparte.

59   COUR DU COMMERCE

— No. 8. In 1792 one of the supervisors of what was at the time a typography of which the facade can still be seen, was Guillaume Brune, previously a printer in Brive and later to become marshal of France. Late in 1792 or early in 1793, the establishment was requisitioned by the Convention and entrusted to Marat, who lived about fifty meters away and printed his newspaper *l'Ami du peuple* there. He and Simone Evrard sold all they owned in order to keep it going. He sanctioned a general system of dispossession and executions which called for the fall of 270,000 heads. The newspaper was printed here until the tribune was assassinated, on July 13, 1793. The typography remained active until these last years. After the Terror the widow of Brissot opened a reading room above, using her late husband's library.

— No. 9. This is where the German Tobias Schmidt, a maker of harpsichords, perfected, in collaboration with Guillotin and Sanson, the first guillotine, and tried it out in the courtyard on sheep. The blade, initially crescent shaped, was finally in slanting form, on the advice, it is said of Louis XVI. . . Guillotin presented the project to the National Assembly, declaring: "The patient will at most feel a slight chill on his neck".

60   HOUSE

10 rue de la Huchette

General Bonaparte, waiting for an assignment, took up lodgings in this house in 1795, in a room that cost him three francs a week. He lived there until 13 Vendémiaire. The balustraded wooden staircase is still the one he used.

THE LATIN QUARTER

PLACE HENRI MONDOR

61

△ **Place Henri Mondor.** The statue of Danton stands on the site of his house. The buildings behind it already existed at the time of the Revolution.

The intersection of the Rue de l'Ecole de Médecine and Boulevard Saint-Germain, now called Place Henri Mondor, is an important Revolutionary site. Actually the opening of the boulevard has wiped out the west end of the Rue de l'Ecole de Médecine, where many of the outstanding figures of the neighbouring club of the Cordeliers lived.

— *Danton*:

The Cour du Commerce on the other side of the Boulevard, extended at the time, with a bend, as far as the Rue des Cordeliers, which it reached passing under the arcade of a house known as Hôtel Molinié. Danton lived here, on the second floor, where his windows looked out on the houses of the south side of the street, which are still there. After 1789 he occupied a large seven-room apartment on the first floor above the mezzanine. His son Antoine ws born here on June 18,1793. When his wife Gabrielle Charpentier died, he married Louise Gely, fifteen years old, three months later. He was arrested here on March 30, 1794 and taken to Luxembourg, the Conciergerie, before the revolutionary Tribunal, and finally to the guillotine. The overpowering monument by Auguste Paris (1891) stands on the site of his house.

— *Marat*:

A stone's throw away, at the corner of the Rue des Cordeliers (de l'Ecole de Médecine) and Rue du Paon, that is towards the east side of the square, was a furnished house known as Hôtel de Cahors. Marat lived on the first floor, overlooking the courtyard, right near his typography. It was here that Charlotte Corday came on July 13,1793. Turned away once in the morning by the concierge, then a second time at the lunch hour by Simone Evrard, the tribune's mistress, she succeeded, on Marat's orders, in gaining admission at her third attempt and, after having exchanged a few words with him, planted her knife into the breast that emerged from the bathtub. Arrested in the antechamber, she was imprisoned in the Conciergerie that night.

— *Simon*:

On the site of the embankment, at the eastern end, was the house (16 Rue des Cordeliers) where the shoemaker Simon lived in 1788, in a wretched lodging on the second floor, composed of a single room on the street and two small closets without windows. Here he met Marie-Jeanne Aladame, forty-three years old, initially maid of all work for a wine merchant who lived across the way, at the corner of what is now Rue Dupuyren, then maid on the second floor of the same house. Simon, who was fifty-two, married her on May 20, 1788. After their marriage, the couple went to live on the third floor of one of the houses that still stand behind the statue, probably the last one on the right. They stayed there until they were taken to the Temple.

FACULTÉ DE MÉDECINE

12 rue de l'Ecole de Médecine

The fall of the monarchy brought in its wake the destruction of the monarchic emblems and of the "images of feudality", and many decorations were modified, often quite skilfully. At the School of Surgery, built sixteen years before, the porch had been decorated by the sculptor Pierre-François Berruer with a relief showing Louis XV ordering the construction of the building. In December 1794, the sculptor, who was still living, replaced the figure of the king with one of Charity, using the arm of Louis XV carved on the adjacent stone. At the same time Minerva lost her ribbon of St. Louis and the diplomas, receiving a spear in exchange, while the crowns that originally spilled from the horn of plenty were replaced by coins. And for good measure the sculptor also added a sheep, an animal one would hardly call revolutionary: transformations that can still be detected today.

▷ **An example of modified decoration.** On the
▽ pediment of the School of Surgery, the figure of Charity replaced that of Louis XV. Her right arm was that of the king.

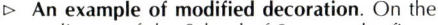

THE CORDELIERS
15 rue de l'Ecole de Médecine

The convent of the Franciscans, known as Cordeliers, founded here in 1230, had mostly been turned over to other uses when the Revolution began. Various services were housed there, in particular, above the north gallery of the cloister, the team of the engineer Verniquet which was busy preparing its famous plan of Paris, and which continued its work throughout the Revolution. The name of Cordeliers had spread to the entire neighborhood. On April 27, 1790, some of the inhabitants, in particular Camille Desmoulins, founded the Société des Amis des Droits de l'Homme et du Citoyen, immediately known as the club of the Cordeliers. They held their meetings in the church of the convent even though it had not yet been completely abandoned, for at the beginning of 1791 Camille Desmoulins and Lucile Duplessis came here to confess to a friar before their marriage.

In May 1791, the club was expelled and moved to Rue Mazarin, then to the Rue Dauphine, while the convent was used for other purposes. Marat, as the local doctor, took care of the Marseillais wounded on August 10th, and the wife of the shoemaker Simon, who lived nearby, moved here to take care of them.

▽ **The cloister of the Cordeliers.**

▽ **The former refectory of the convent of the Cordeliers**, where some of the sessions of the famous club were held.

The club of the Cordeliers with its three to four hundred members returned to the convent in the month of Pluviôse year II (January-February 1793). It is not known precisely where their meetings were held at the time: perhaps once more in the church, in the sacristy, or it may be, after the spring of 1793, in the refectory which is still standing. The old walls of the convent echoed with the exhortations and oaths of Desmoulins, Danton, Hébert, Chaumette, Legendre, Marat, who was assassinated in his house, across the way, on July 13, 1793. His body was laid out in the convent church and then, after having been carried through the streets of Paris together with his bathtub, buried under a tumulus of rocks in the convent garden (southeast of where the Faraboeuf amphitheater is now), before being transferred, on September 21, 1794, to the Panthéon.

After Marat's death, the club survived for a few months, dominated by Hébert and Vincent and adopting an ultra-revolutionary approach. On March 24, 1794, the execution of the Hébertists was the beginning of the end for the club, and that of the Dantonists, ten days later, precipitated its dissolution. On March 30, 1794, the refectory was requisitioned and turned into a storeroom for all the libraries confiscated from the *émigrés* and the condemned prisoners. Even so a few die-hards remained, such as Simon and his wife, who had left the Temple and had settled into small lodgings in the convent in July of 1794. The evening of Thermidor 9 the former shoemaker

△ Door of the refectory of the Cordeliers.

64 HOUSE OF DESMOULINS

2 place de l'Odéon

After their marriage (December 29, 1790), Camille and Lucile Desmoulins went to live in this house, on the second floor above the mezzanine, at the corner of the Rue Crebillon. It was here, on March 20, 1794, that they came to arrest Camille, taking him straight to the prison of Luxembourg. At the corner of the theater of the Odéon he turned one last time to see Lucile weeping at the window. She was also arrested a few days later.

△ **Place de l'Odéon**. Camille and Lucile Desmoulins lived in this house on the Place de l'Odéon (3rd storey, windows with roller blinds).

appeared before the members of the club and tried to galvanize them into action in aid of Robespierre. No one heeded his appeal and the journalist Fiévée had him arrested. The next day he was guillotined.

The club was dissolved in January 1795, when demolition of the church began. Moreover, in November 1794, a law turned the former convent over to the school of medicine across the way. In June of 1796 the "Hôpital des Cliniques" was installed here.

The only thing still standing of what was one of the most important sites of the Revolution is the lovely flamboyant Gothic refectory built between the end of the 14th and the end of the 16th centuries, situated near the entrance (note the picturesque caretaker's house) and recently restored. The road along the south facade still has the aspect of a country lane it had two centuries ago. Nothing is left of the church, which lay in the roadway of the street, except the south eaves wall, recognizable only by the thickness of the passageways which join the laboratories set at the outskirts of the street with the north gallery of the cloister. As for the latter, it was rebuilt in the 19th century, but on the same ground plan, with the same foundations and in part the same old stones. Lastly the old houses at numbers 11, 13, and 15 of Rue de l'Ecole de Médecine were convent annexes and no. 15 still has a fine vaulted wine cellar (cave).

65 HOUSE

15 rue Servandoni

When the Girondins were accused, Condorcet, who was suspect, hid himself here from July 10, 1793 on, at the house of the widow of the painter Vernet, and there wrote one of his most remarkable works, *Esquisse des progres de l'esprit humain*. Afraid of further compromising his hostess, he left on March 25, 1794, and encountered death in Bourg-la-Reine three days later.

CHURCH OF SAINT-SULPICE

On December 19, 1790, Camille and Lucile Desmoulins were married here with Robespierre as their witness. In 1793, the church became the Temple of Reason, then temple of Victory for the Théophilanthropes. Their great pontefix, La Revellière-Lepaux, presided over the offices. The building was transformed into a storeroom for fodder under the Directory, but cleared out for the great banquet with seven hundred guests offered on 15 Brumaire year VII to Generals Bonaparte and Moreau.

▷ **Saint-Sulpice as it is today.** The facade was freed, after the Revolution, by the demolition of the Seminary, which stood on the site of the square.

▽ **Reception Given at Saint-Sulpice in Honor of General Bonaparte and General Moreau on 15 Brumaire year VII** (engraving by Charles Motte, Cabinet des Estampes).

LES CARMES
Rue de Vaugirard

In 1611, the Carmelites had set up their headquarters in the Rue de Vaugirard almost out in the country. The Revolution found them popular in the district, thanks to their charity. Despite the official suppression of the convent, many of the monks remained, trusting to their good reputation, and gave shelter to their brothers from the right bank, who had abandoned their convent of Marais. After August 11, 1792, a certain number of ecclesiastic prisoners who did not belong to the order were interned here — prelates, Robertins from Vaugirard, seminarians from Issy. They were shut up in the church, under the surveillance of the National Guard: the altarpiece from the high altar, with its painting by Quentin Varin and its columns in black marble, is evidence of a captivity that was religious in more ways than one, both for the building and for its inmates.

The fury of September 2nd fell on this house, half convent and half prison. The sites of the massacre include the

▷ **Convent of the Carmes: the site of the massacre.** "Judget" in the corridor behind, the victims then left through this door. The slaughterers were posted at either side, on the stairs. On the steps, a plaque: *Hic ceciderunt.*

▽ **The remains of the victims.** The bones found in 1867 in the excavations in the garden are to be seen in the crypt.

garden, where the inmates were walking that day and which was invaded by a band of rioters who killed everyone they met. The archbishop of Arles fell riddled by blows and a score of priests were killed in the oratory at the back of the garden. But four or five young friars, with the aid of a stone statue of a monk, succeeded in climbing the enclosing wall: statue and wall are still there. It was then that the porter Maillard appeared at the window with the rusty grate that can still be seen and, with a pale face, cried:

— Wait! Don't be in such a hurry to kill them, they must be tried first!

Maillard, before leaving for another massacre, at the Abbey, had a table set up in the atrium, at the foot of the stairs that led to the monks' cells. The prisoners, once more shut up in the church, were called two by two. Crossing the sacristy, they appeared before the tribunal, where three answers settled their fate. This atrium, a mockery of justice, both as site and in the sentences pronounced, is still there, as is the corridor on the garden side that leads to the door, which, in three hours, was opened about eighty times to let pass the wretched prisoners, for whom a mob of assassins, their sleeves rolled up above their bloody arms, was waiting. The small worn steps are also still intact. An inscription of two words has been added: *Hic ceciderunt*.

Most of the victims were killed there, on those steps sticky with blood, and the denuded corpses were then thrown into the garden. Here, as at the Abbey, murder became even more horrible for it was perpetrated in a sacred place.

The opening of the Rue de Rennes, in 1867, did away with the oratory at the back of the garden: the crypt received the altar, the pavement and various fragments of blood-stained wainscoting. The statue of the Virgin that was also at the back of the garden and which was the last thing some of the victims saw has been set alongside.

At the center of the enclosure is a column which marks the spot where the first victim, the Abbot Giraud, fell. In the building, the "room of the swords" still preserves the faded signs of the bloody pikes. We will come back to this room.

In 1867 excavations at the center of the garden brought to light an old abandoned well, into which about ninety corpses had been thrown, and which then had been filled with everything the grave diggers could lay their hands on: remnants of meals, brooms, glasses, bottles, gardener's bells, jam and pharmacy jars, rusted spades which looked as if they were bloody. The crypt was prepared to receive these relics, and in a rather theatrical

▽ **A view of the garden of the Carmelites.**

presentation, various cases contain the principal bones, broken crania and jaw bones. The floor in the crypt consists of earth taken from the well and a few plaques of black marble bear 117 names.

During the massacre the Carmelites, who had been closed in the attic, were spared. They soon scattered and the building became a country dance hall, under the name of Bal des Tilleuls, later Bal des Zephyrs. This did not last long, for the Terror once more needed prisons.

The new inmates began to arrive in December 1793. In particular, the Marquis de Sade, the Comte de Soyecourt, the Countess de Jarnac, the Duchess de Richelieu, but also ordinary people, servants, and Guillaume Loison, puppeteer of the Guignol in the Champs-Elysées. As well as the "general" Santerre, who had left service some time before and, in March 1794, the Girondin deputy Rouzet, whom we will later meet again at the Belhomme pension. That same month two famous figures, the Prince de Salm, for whom the town house which bears his name had been built and General Alexandre de Beauharnais. Since the general's wife Josephine had made overtures in an attempt to have him pardoned, she was sent to keep him company, and her name is still written in the room of the swords, with below the inscription incised by a prisoner:

— Oh Liberty, when will you cease being an empty word? Seventeen days have passed since we were shut up here; they told us we would leave tomorrow; but is this not a vain hope?

During their confinement the Beauharnais were reconciled, but this did not stop the general from falling in love with the beautiful Delphine de Sabran, who shared Josephine's cell. On her part, Josephine had an affair with General Hoche, imprisoned after March 20th (30 Ventôse year II) in a room nearby, where a cellmate of his wrote French and Latin proverbs on the wall in an elegant calligraphy, still to be seen.

Frédéric de Salm and Beauharnais left the Carmelites on 5 Thermidor (July 23, 1794) for the revolutionary tribune, which condemned them to death. Before leaving for the scaffold, the former had written to his sister, entrusting her with his son. Later she bought the land of Picpus. When the prison was closed, the convent was put up for sale and bought by a speculator who, in 1798, opened the Rue d'Assas, eliminating part of the garden. But the work of renewal had already begun the year before. A former Carmelite nun, Camille de Soyecourt, daughter of the nobleman who had been guillotined, had reconstituted a small community and, from August 15, 1797 on, began to redeem the convent. She had it restored and occupied it together with other nuns, taking as her own the small room where her father had been confined and where she lived for forty-eight years.

RUE MADAME AND RUE DE FLEURUS

The economic slump of the last years of the Reign slowed down the building boom in Paris but the events of 1789 did not bring it to a complete halt and building speculation continued for some time. This was when the count of Provence, brother of the king, parcelled out the east part of the Luxembourg gardens where new streets now named Rue Madame, Rue de Fleurus (denomination of 1798), Rue Jean Bart and Rue Duguay-Trouin were traced in 1790. Some of the buildings still date to that period. The oldest seems to be the one at 57-59 Rue Madame, still in Louis XVI style with its mezzanine topped by a piano nobile with stone balconies and its vestibule (at no. 59) framed by fine Doric columns supporting a frieze. Number 9 Rue de Fleurus still has its refined Louis XVI architecture, the lanceolate window grates and the molded doorway. To be noted also numbers 16, 18, 26 Rue de Fleurus, and 51 Rue Madame.

▽ Rue de Fleurus as it is now.

PALAIS DU LUXEMBOURG

At the end of Louis XVI's reign, the Palais du Luxembourg belonged in appanage to the count of Provence, the king's brother, who lived there until June 20, 1791, the day of his flight. The hôtel was confiscated and, in July 1793, transformed into a prison under the name of Maison nationale de Sûreté. The Girondins were its first inmates, followed by eight hundred other persons of whom more than a third were decapitated. Among the victims, the Marshal de Noailles, his wife, the Viscountess de Noailles, Hébert, Danton, Camille Desmoulins, Hérault de Séchelles.

Family members communicated with the prisoners by means of gestures from the garden, but the committee of Sûreté Général had the rope barrier put further and further back until the prisoners could see their dear ones only if they had binoculars. We can imagine Camille Desmoulins in the room where he was shut up, in the mezzanine of the west wing, almost crouching at a low window so he could see his wife pass back and forth, their child in her arms. "Lucile", he wrote, "oh my dear Lucile, yesterday evening my heart broke when I saw your mother in the garden. I saw how she suffered from her handkerchief, from the veil she lowered. When you come back, have her sit a bit closer, so I can see you both better. My binoculars are not good...".

On 9 Thermidor, Robespierre, arrested on order of the Convention, was brought to Luxembourg, but the astounded porter refused to accept him and for the tribune this was the beginning of his last adventure. In the weeks that followed Choderlos de Laclos was imprisoned here, and the painter David, also lodged in the mezzanine, perhaps in the same room as Desmoulins, who had implored him in vain. Here he sketched the *Rape of the Sabines* and from this window he painted a corner of the garden — the avenue of plane-trees with its fence: the only landscape in his oeuvre. Joseph Le Bon, the slaughterer of Arras and Cambrai, was also here, leaving only for his trial.

In 1795 the prison was suppressed and the palace turned over to the Directory, which held its sessions here. One of the Five Directors, Barras, set himself up here with sumptuous furniture, whose origins can easily be imagined, and gave splendid receptions. This is probably where the young General Bonaparte met Josephine. On December 10, 1797 (20 Primaire year VI), after the treaty of Campo Formio, he returned here to the Directory.

The other four Directors more modestly settled into the Petite Luxembourg, where Nicolas Sadi Carnot, son of Lazare Carnot and later to become the inventor of ther-

▽ **The front door of the Palace of Luxembourg**. A prison under the Terror, the palace thereafter became the headquarters for the Directory.

△ **A Session of the Directory in Full Dress on 30 Brumaire year IV** (engraving by Berthault, Musée Carnavalet). The scene takes place in the palace of Luxembourg. The ministers are seated at the sides. In the center, the five Directors, including the president.

modynamics, was born on June I, 1796.
On 18 Brumaire year VIII three hundred soldiers commanded by General Moreau penetrated Luxembourg while Barras was taking a bath: the Revolution was over.

The communs of Luxembourg

This annex (36 Rue de Vaugirard) was in communication with the palace by means of an underground passage, and the Commune refused to imprison the royal family in the Palais du Luxembourg for fear of an attempt at flight. In 1795, the office of weights and measures was installed here, which is why there is a marble meterstick under the arcading, of which the story must be told.
On May 8, 1790, the Constituent Assembly had commissioned the Academy of Sciences, including Monge, Laplace and Lavoisier, with the preparation of a new system of weights and measures. It was proposed to take the ten millionth part of a quarter of the terrestrial meridian as the basic unit. On 12 Thermidor year I (August 1, 1793), the Convention adopted the principle of the meter and, on 18 Germinal year III (April 8, 1795) the metric system was instituted. Three days later the Bureau of Weights and Measures was created and installed here. The scope of the bureau was to acquaint the Parisians with the new system and put the model at their disposition. Various meter sticks, designed by Chalgrin and cut from blocks of marble from Marly, were set up in sixteen sites in Paris between February 1796 and May 1799. One of these is still on the facade of the Bureau and another one is at the Ministry of Justice.

The Luxembourg Gardens

When the count of Provence, future Louis XVII, took possession of the estate of Luxembourg, the gardens were not at all as they are today. They stretched out much further east and the prince, in the latter years of his reign, decided to cut up the part on this side into lots, an apportionment which continued throughout the Revolution.
On the south side, however, the gardens bordered with the convent of the Chartreuse which blocked the view and although it was suppressed in 1790, the monastic buildings remained standing. The Convention then decided to tear them down and to enlarge the gardens, but this was not put into effect until the Directory. The old enclosure was demolished in Primaire year IV (November-December 1795), and at the price of much terracing, the prospect on an axis with the palace was lengthened and framed by flower beds as far as the observatory. This lovely landscaping was a result of the Revolution.

THE PANTHEON

The new church of the Abbey Sainte-Geneviève, built by Soufflot, had not yet been finished when the Revolution broke out. The architect had died in 1780 and his work was being continued by his pupils, Brebion and Rondelet, who finished the dome in 1790. The next year, on April 4th, after the death of Mirabeau the Constituent Assembly decided to transform the building into a Pantheon, for the tombs of the glories of the nation, and the famous inscription: *Aux grands hommes la Patrie reconnaissante* was their doing. In other words it was an attempt to create a new Saint-Denis for the new regime.

▷ **The Panthéon as it is now.** When the church of Sainte-Geneviève was transformed into the Panthéon the windows were walled up.

▽ **Apotheosis of Rousseau, Transferral of his Mortal Remains to the Panthéon on October 11, 1794** (engraving by Berthault, Musée Carnavalet).

△ **Transferral of the Ashes of Voltaire to the Panthéon** (Prieur, drawing, Musée Carnavalet). The procession passes near the Pont Royal.

The famous theoretician Quatremère de Quincy was entrusted with adapting the building to its new destination. He therefore decided, late in 1792, to eliminate the two steeples of the apse, forty meters high, and wall up the forty-two windows which, it was said at the time, bestowed "an air of hilarity" on the building. Traces can still be seen. The rather forbidding aspect of the facade, which Soufflot would not have approved, is due to the Revolutionary regime. At the top of the dome, the cross was to have been replaced by a gigantic figure of Fame, by Dejoux.

Sculptural decoration of the period, still extant inside, includes the rosettes and the lozenges of the dome, which replaced the flowers, ears of wheat and heads of cherubs originally there, while the winged animals in the squinches of the first bay of the nave symbolize Philosophy, Virtue, the Sciences and Genius.

On the facade, under the porch, the two bas reliefs at either end, both dating to 1793, can still be seen. They depict *Patriotic Devotion* by Chaudet and *Public Instruction* by Lesueur.

After the building was transformed, the supposed mortal remains of Voltaire were buried here (July 12, 1791), as was the body of Mirabeau (December 13, 1791) and that of Le Peletier de Saint-Fargeau (January 24, 1793). But when Mirabeau's intrigues with the royal family were discovered he was "depantheonized" on September 21, 1794, and the "virtuous" Marat was buried in his place. The Thermidor reaction thus rendered to the tribune that honor which Robespierre had refused him. On October 11, 1794, the remains of Jean-Jacques Rousseau were buried here, and on the following February 26th, the bodies of Marat and Le Peletier were expelled. The two philosophers remained.

The famous tombs of Voltaire and Rousseau date to this period, both in their provvisory state, in wood, without ever being executed in marble. The former is decorated with garlands, antique masks and urns, while the latter has a small *trompe l'oeil* door on the front, open just enough to let a hand holding a torch pass through, with the famous inscription "*Ici repose l'homme de la Nature et de la Vérité*".

71 CAFÉ
2 rue des Fossés Saint-Jacques

This cafe with its railing still looks very much the way it did two centuries ago. The letters *St* in the two inscriptions of street names on the plaques at the corner were scraped away during the Revolution. They were later restored, but this correction is still noticeable.

▽ **Panthéon**, statue and tomb of Voltaire.

72 — CAFÉ
40 rue de la Montagne Sainte-Geneviève

This cafe still has the iron grilles it had at the time. Called "A la ci-devant Geneviève", it was the rendezvous of the sansculottes of the district.

73 — SAINT-NICOLAS DU CHARDONNET
23 rue des Bernardins

This is another example of the transformation of ornamentation that at the time of the Revolution was judged seditious. In the 17th century, the sculptor Legendre had decorated the watersheds of the pediment of the side portal with figures of angels carrying the cross of Christ and the crozier of St. Nicholas. These religious attributes were replaced by revolutionary pikes.

74 — COLLÈGE DES BERNARDINS
24 rue de Poissy

Suppressed in 1790, this monastic establishment, of which the fine refectory is still extant, was transformed into a warehouse for meal and a prison for convicts. At the time of the September massacres, the sansculottes of the neighborhood thought the seventy-three convicts were aristocratic friars in disguise and, with the exception of three, they were all massacred.

75 — COLLÈGE DES ECOSSAIS
65 rue du Cardinal Lemoine

In the 14th century a foundation to allow Scotch students to come and work in Paris was created. In the 17th century they were boarded in the large building, erected between 1662 and 1665, which is still extant.
The college was closed by the Revolution and under the Terror was transformed into a prison which momentarily housed the famous Belhomme and where Saint-Just was imprisoned for a few hours on 9 Thermidor. But as foreign property the building was not sold, and was later returned to the Church of England. The portal with the thistle of Scotland above is still the one that Saint-Just crossed one torrid day in July.

▽ **Church of Saint-Nicolas du Chardonnet.** The angels on the church were provided with Revolutionary pikes.

△ **Port Royal as it is today**. Very little has changed since the times of the Terror.

▽ **The house on the Rue Jean Dolent**.

76 — PORT-ROYAL
123 boulevard de Port-Royal

The old convent of Port-Royal in Paris, closed in 1790, was rebaptised Port-libre and soon transformed... into a prison, through which many, including Malesherbes, Mlle de Sombreuil, Florian, passed. Then on 9 Thermidor, Couthon. Two gendarmes came to free him on order of the Commune and he left for the Hôtel de Ville. In 1796 the Directory set up the *Maison de l'allaitement* here, a forebear of the present-day lying-in hospital.

77 — HOUSE
23 rue Jean Dolent

This charming small house (known as "de Montrouge" situated outside the enclosure of Ledoux) property of the Duke of Biron, seems to have been where the partisans of the Duc d'Orléans met at the beginning of the Revolution and where the projects for the *cahiers de doléances*, involving the possessions of the d'Orléans, were drawn up by Choderlos de Laclos and Siéyès.

THE SALPÊTRIÈRE

47 boulevard de l'Hôpital

On September 3, 1792, the hospital of the Salpêtrière was stormed by a band of more than two hundred armed men, including numerous pimps and bullies. They broke into the dormitory of the "Commun" where the prostitutes rounded up in the streets of Paris were interned and let them out.

"The scene had to be seen to be believed," Restif was to write in his *Les nuits de Paris*. "It was not bloody but nothing as obscene was ever had. All those hapless women offered their liberators or the first-come what they called their maidenhead...". Many of them were freed at that price.

The day after, the courtyards were crowded both by the pimps and bullies of the preceding evening, who boasted of their exploits, as well as by girls who had come to settle accounts with the various idlers. The director, preoccupied, asked for aid, but Pétion, the mayor of Paris, could not be found anywhere, and Santerre, commander of the National Guard, did nothing. Late in the afternoon, the hospital was invaded by a band of armed men provenant from Bicêtre where they had massacred 164 prisoners. They forced the director to hand over the admission ledgers and set themselves up in the old kitchen overlooking the courtyard now known as that of "the September massacres", near the building of "La Force". For two hours these improvised judges examined the list of eighty-seven names, interrupting their work just long enough every now and then to down another glass of wine, and decided to proceed according to age.

They began at seven in the evening by torchlight. The first four prisoners were freed but the fifth, seventy-one years old, was hit over the head in the courtyard, then finished off with bayonets. Desrues, the widow of a poisoner who had died on the scaffold, had been condemned for life. She was forty-seven years old at the time, and tried to save herself but she was hit over the head, finished off, then raped. During the night thirty-five women were killed and fifty-two were liberated.

"If only you knew the details", Mme Roland was to write, "of that expedition! The women brutally raped before being torn to pieces by those tigers, their insides drawn out in ribbons, the bloody human flesh eaten! You know of my enthusiasm for the Revolution: but at this point, I am ashamed".

The Commune of Paris itself was aghast at this slaughter and sent the shoemaker Simon to try and stop the massacre, but he could do nothing.

At dawn the slaughterers, covered with blood and wine, invaded the building of the young girls, and raped them. In December 1794, the prison of Salpêtrière was definitely closed and the building set aside for the role of assistance it still holds.

Another Revolutionary figure, Théroigne de Méricourt, who had lost her mind, was interned here where she died in 1817. The courtyard Saint-Vincent de Paul is, as we have said, traditionally called the courtyard of the September massacre, but some set the site in the Franklin courtyard. Probably the massacres took place in various parts of the building.

△ **Salpêtrière**, courtyard of the September massacres.

JARDIN DES PLANTES

Place Valhubert

The Revolution transformed the old royal Botanical Gardens into the Museum of Natural History (decree of the Convention, June 10, 1793) and put it under the direction of Bernardin de Saint-Pierre. A menagerie was created, with the animals which had survived from that of the king in Versailles, in particular a superb rhinocerous. In 1795, when he conquered Holland, General Pichegru seized two elephants of the Stadthouder and sent them here, where they made a great sensation.

LA NATION

THE GUILLOTINE AND ITS LAST ITINERARY

When the scaffold was first transferred to the Bastille and then to Place du Trône renversé, the tumbrils, after crossing the Pont au Change, turned right instead of left, as before, and began an even longer journey: the Quai des Gesvres, Place de Grève, arcade Saint-Jean which led to Place Saint-Gervais, Rue François Miron, then from the church of Saint-Paul-Saint Louis on, the interminable route which, from Rue "Antoine", the Bastille and "Faubourg Antoine" led to the Place du Trône renversé. Along this itinerary flanked here and there by buildings, at times almost out in the open countryside, the procession was occasionally accompanied by cries of derision, but frequently made its way in an atmosphere of resignation or indifference.

Often, when it passed the church of Saint-Paul, a few priests might be encountered on the steps, intermingled with the crowd and wearing the *carmagnole*, discreetly voicing an absolution as the tumbril passed: the chaplains of the guillotine. On 4 Thermidor (July 22) the Abbot Carrichon, chaplain of the de Noailles family, was in the street dressed in blue with a red jacket. In the confusion resulting from an unexpected downpour he succeeded in drawing near the cart which carried the Duchess d'Ayen, the Viscountess de Noailles and Marshal de Noailles: they saw him as he lifted his hand in sign of absolution.

On July 17, the sixteen Carmelites of Compiègne covered this route, singing the *Miserere*, which silenced the outcries. Many of the houses now on Rues François Miron, Saint-Antoine, in the Faubourg Saint'Antoine, date to before this time and therefore witnessed the passage of these processions of death.

On 9 Thermidor something happened on this street, between Saint-Paul and the Bastille, which is oft repeated. The convoy of prisoners was on its way to the scaffold, when an indistinct murmer began to be heard above the noise — something was changing. In the Rue Saint-Antoine, the crowd, tired of blood and more or less consciously already anxious for a change, stopped the convoy, asking for pardon and even went so far as to unhitch the horses. They cried to the prisoners to flee but they hesitated. Resigned to death they were no longer capable of grasping the fleeting tail of Fortune as she flashed by. Armed troops, commanded by Hanriot, soon caught up with the crowd, order was reestablished and respect for the official sentence imposed. The forty-six prisoners, the last of the regime, once more set out for the guillotine.

△ **The faubourg Saint-Antoine as it is today.** Many of these houses already existed at the time of the Terror.

CHURCH OF SAINTE-MARGUERITE

40 rue Saint-Bernard

At the time this church was the headquarters of an immense parish, comprising several tens of thousands of inhabitants. The Temple fell under its jurisdiction and this is why, on June 10, 1795, the Dauphin Louis XVII was buried in the small parish cemetery still in use at the time when many an old cemetery in Paris, adjacent to its church, had been closed and remained empty in the latter years of the reign and the early years of the Revolution. With a fine cross of 1717 rising up over it, it was used until 1804 and not until 1894 was a modest tomb raised above the remains of the child. Thereafter, the cemetery was demolished for the construction, on the street, of a kindergarten, and most of the tombstones were eliminated.

There is still something moving about the site which now serves as a playground for children. Upon arriving at the church, ask for the guardian priest, and go along the external wall of the building as far as the enclosure, which flanks the chapel of the Souls in Purgatory and the north crossing of the transept. The tomb, framed by cypresses, is on the right, against the wall: a small stone cross, marked *LXVII 1785-1795* is set above an extremely simple stone engraved with this inscription: *Attendite et videte si est dolor sicut dolor meus* (Stop, and ask yourselves if there is sorrow such as mine). After all sorts of suppositions, it seems most probable, in particular after the excavations of 1979, that the Dauphin died at the Temple and that he was buried here.

Immediately to the right is a tombstone on which the Revolutionary calendar is united to religious piety: "Here lie the citizens Boulon father and son, merchants of wood at the Rapée, who died on 11 Vendémiaire and 29 Messidor year II. De profundis".

The cross of 1717 is still there, with a few extant tombstones.

△ **Fountain** which was at the center of the riots of April 1789.

THE REVOLT OF THE MANUFACTURE REVEILLON

Reveillon, a famous manufacturer of wallpaper, had his factory in the Faubourg Saint-Antoine, on the site of 31, Rue de Montreuil. As a result of an ambiguous and imprudent declaration, on his part, his workers thought their employer had announced a cut in wages, as prices were rising. The result was a revolt on April 26, 1789: after two days of meetings and clamor, the rioters succeeded in entering the factory, which was sacked, but the repression was ferocious: there may have been as many as three hundred dead, many more than in the taking of the Bastille. But, neither among the dead, nor among the forty-six arrested, were there any employees of the factory. The whole thing was a frame-up.

The fountain of 1719 situated at the intersection of Faubourg Saint-Antoine and Rue de Montreuil was at the center of the revolt and can be seen in the engravings of the time which illustrate it. The fountain is still there.

◁ **The tomb of Louis XVII** in the cemetery of Sainte-Marguerite.

PLACE DU TRÔNE RENVERSÉ
Place de la Nation

During the Revolution Place du Trône, whose name dates to Louis XIV, became Place du Trône renversé (of the upturned throne). Then as now, it was occupied by Ledoux's customs house, composed of two pavilions and two sentry boxes with columns above, but there were only a few houses around, and broad open spaces. The scaffold, previously in the Bastille, was erected here on 16 Prairial (June 14, 1794) and the victims of that first day were buried in the cemetery of Sainte-Marguerite. This solution was however purely temporary for the cemetery was too small and the inhabitants of the district protested. It was then that the old convent of Picpus came to mind.

After this, the mechanism of death worked uninterruptedly for six weeks. The scaffold had been set up at the edge of the square, between the Boulevard de Picpus and what is now Avenue du Bel-Air. The procession, which came from the Palais de Justice by the itinerary previously described, arrived late in the afternoon and the condemned prisoners, hauled down from the tumbril, were lined up with their backs to the scaffold, separated from the rare spectators by a semicircle of guards. The headsman Sanson at the time wore a work smock over his city clothes and his helpers went at it with skill and discipline. One by one as each prisoner mounted the steps, he was propped on the plank which was lowered, and the lunette was dropped down over his neck, soon followed by the dull swish of the blade. Bodies and heads, dripping blood, were thrown on the cart set alongside the scaffold, a heavy wagon, lined with lead, and painted red. As night fell, it set out for Picpus, loaded with from twenty to forty mutilated corpses, pulled by two Percherons, enveloped by the horrible odor that emanated from the decapitated bodies. There were fifty-four executions on 29 Prairial (in twenty-four minutes, for which Barère proposed Sanson for a premium), fifty-five on 5 Thermidor, thirty-seven on the 7th, fifty-two on the 8th, and forty-six on the 9th. All in all thirteen hundred and six victims in six weeks.

Among these was the Abbot de Fénelon, eighty years old, founder of the Oeuvre des Petits Savoyards, worshipped by his young chimney sweeps, who in vain had asked that he be pardoned. When they accompanied him to the scaffold on July 7th, the priest asked Sanson for one last grace. — Untie my hands so I can bless these young ones. The executioner agreed and the abbot traced a large sign of the cross in the air. There were many, among those present, who fell to their knees.

On 29 Messidor (July 12) it was the sixteeen Carmelites of Compiègne who, at the foot of the scaffold, lifted their voices in the *Veni Creator*. The song died with the last of them.

On 7 Thermidor, André Chénier met another poet, Antoine Roucher, in his tumbril and greeted him, it is said, with the first lines of the *Andromaque*

— Yes, for once more find I a friend so faithful.

The head, still full of masterpieces, of the author of the *Iambes*, rolled in the setting sun. Roucher was the last to die: he had seen the blade fall thirty-six times.

▽ **The Place de la Nation as it is today**. The architect Ledoux had built pavilions and sentry houses for the collection of customs taxes (octroi), which the Revolution eliminated for a period of time.

PICPUS

35 rue de Picpus

The canonnesses, Dames of Saint-Augustin, had set up their convent with its large garden here in 1642 and were expulsed in May 1792. The chapel was torn down while the property was confiscated and rented to a certain Riedain who used it as a vegetable garden. But in December 1793, his neighbor Coignard, who owned a private clinic at the corner of what is now the Boulevard Diderot and the Rue de Picpus, made him a proposal. This clinic was like the one run by Belhomme where inmates might be admitted, using either influence or money, and be protected from the guillotine. Requests rose as the Terror was intensifed and Coignard needed more room. Riedain agreed to sublet the buildings and garden, keeping one pavilion for himself. Thus from February 1794 on, the former convent witnessed the arrival of new inmates including Coignard's rival, Belhomme, who had profitted from the situation and was arrested, but who also knew better than anyone else how to overcome the inclemency of the official prisons. Among the others who arrived were Volney, the author of *Méditations sur les Révolutions*, the Duke of Brancas-Villars and his wife. This small world lived in relative tranquility until the day, 26 Prairial (June 14, 1794), when two officials appeared with an order to visit the place. Riedain received them amiably and showed them the buildings and the garden with the pride of a man who had made a good investment. The following day he observed with astonishment as thirty-four laborers set to work at the back of the enclosure, breaking through the north wall, chopping down fruit trees, and digging two pits which a palisade separated from the rest of the garden, which was left to his boarders. Riedain indignantly protested, first to the master masons, then to the authorities of the district, and finally to the Convention offices, which required considerable courage, but all in vain. The guillotine, of which the Parisians of the center had tired, had been transferred the day before to the Place du Trône renversé, a cemetery was needed and the property confiscated from the church belonged to the Nation. The evening of 27 Prairial one of the pits received its first load of corpses and the opening in the wall was supplied with a

▽ **Cemetery of Picpus, site of the two pits**. At the center is the monument to the memory of the Prince de Salm.

carriage gateway which the blacksmith Ferrière furnished with "a strong chain, a strong wall hook and a lock with three keys".
At this point, every evening at dusk the lead-lined cart painted red and piled high with mutilated corpses left the Place du Trône reversé, skirted the wall which bordered the Fermiers généraux along the internal "chemin de ronde" (Boulevard de Picpus), cutting across the fields, until it reached what is now number 42 Avenue de Saint-Mandé where, at the back of the lot, a gate opened to let it pass: traces can still be seen.
Rainstorms of June often rendered this route more difficult: the wheels of the cart sank down into the muddy soil and more than once extra teams of horses had to be requisitioned. Some evenings, the transferral lasted over an hour.
Once the carriage gate was closed the macabre rite of denuding the corpses began. Installed in a small cave, originally used as a chapel by the nuns, the servants of the guillotine took the shoes off the mutilated corpses, stripped them of their bloody clothes and prepared the list of clothing which they then sold, pocketing the money, until a new rule deprived them of that benefice. Once denuded, the corpses were piled into the pits, packed as tight as possible with the decapitated heads filling up the empty spaces, and without adding lime, to make the most of what room there was. Despite this, in a month, the ditches, one measuring thirty square meters and the other forty, were filled and a third ditch was begun near the entrance gate. But on 9 Thermidor the last of the victims of the Terror were taken to Picpus and, the day after, the guillotine was dismantled.
The carriage gate stayed closed, and Coignard's last inmates lived in the midst of the suffocating stench that had spread throughout the district. Raymond de Sèze, former advocate of Louis XVI, interned here after the spring of 1794, wrote to his family: "From my prison, I breathe the terrible odors of the charnel house of Picpus".
Closed on 5 Brumaire (October 26), the next year the

△ **Picpus, La Fayette's tomb.** The descendents of the dead of Picpus have preserved the right to be buried side by side with the victims.

△ **The enclosure of death.** Fragmentary reconstruction of the palisade which fenced in the enclosure of the victims.

Princess of Hohenzollern, sister of the Prince of Salm whose remains had been laid to rest here, bought the land in which the pits were situated. Eventually other descendents of the victims followed her example and set up a cemetery near the enclosure, in the guardianship of nuns. They are still there, keeping watch over the site, and two centuries later it is still extraordinarily moving.
Crossing the entrance courtyard, a small 17th-century pavilion on the left may be the one in which Riedain lived. Once past the gate, the cemetery lies at the back of the nuns' garden, still as peaceful and serene as it once was. The tombs of the descendents of the victims, which include the greatest names of the French nobility, are here. At the back, a gate, which is opened only in rare occasions, leads to the enclosure of the victims, where the two pits are marked by stone cippi. This is where 1306 bodies have been laid to rest — 1109 men and 197 women: aristocrats, magistrates, priests, Carmelites of Compiègne, but also common people. Outside the cemetery, at the back of the garden, are the reconstructed remains of the palisade erected on 17 Prairial, the site of the grotto where the corpses were stripped, the outlines of the third pit, which was never used, and, above all, in the enclosing wall, the site of the carriage gateway, with the oak architrave still in situ. There are few places, in Paris, as haunting as this.

THE BELHOMME BOARDING HOUSE
157 rue de Charonne

This building stands on the area of Jacques Belhomme's famous clinic about which so many legends have sprung up, lately rectified by M. Vincienne in his studies. In 1770 a private hospital for the feeble minded was created here by Belhomme, a former mirror-vendor. For a long time the doctor in charge was the famous Pinel and paying guests were accepted, both upon request of the police and of the families. During the Terror, those who could, either through money or influence, had themselves transferred to the various private hospitals of Paris. Clients arrived at the Belhomme clinic in ever greater numbers, including Mlle Lang, the advocate Linguet, the Duchess of Gramont and the Duchess of Chatelet, who were all executed, the magistrate Le Peletier de Morfontaine, and Belhomme had to annex the neighboring town house, which belonged to Chabanais, and its garden.

The guests payed a pension of from two to three hundred *livres*, which was not by any means exaggerated. Despite what has been said, it does not appear that any of them had to move to a normal prison and then on to the guillotine because they had exhausted their resources. On January 28, 1794 (9 Pluviôse) Belhomme himself was arrested "for extorsion with regards to the wealthy, and dishumanity towards the unfortunate", and interned in another private hospital, at Picpus from where he was transferred on 11 Germinal year II (March 31, 1794) to the Conciergerie, later condemned to six years in chains (May 22, 1794). But eight days after 9 Thermidor, he managed to have the sentence anulled and was liberated by the court of Versailles on September 7, 1794. He returned to his house where he remained until his death. It was in this second period that the Duchess of Orléans, widow of Philippe Egalité, was here, and the deputy Rouzet, who fell passionately in love with her, and with whom she lived to the end of her life.

The private hospital existed up to 1971, and only afterwards, despite the protests from the Commission du Vieux Paris, were the buildings on the street torn down and replaced by a large structure. Behind it the large garden, completely transformed into a public park, still exists. At the back, the "Pavillon Colbert" still stands in the shade of a large linden tree, the last extant building of the institution, and even this was remodelled in the 19th century. This graceful construction framed by stairs and with its typical rooftops, was used, according to tradition, as chapel by the hospital.

▽ **Surviving building of the Pension Belhomme**.

THE LEADING FIGURES OF THE REVOLUTION

Bailly Jean Sylvain (1736-1793)

Astronomer, elected to the estates-general, he presided over the proceedings in the Tennis Court (Jeu de Paume) on June 20, 1789. Elected mayor of Paris, after the fall of the Bastille he received Louis XVI at the Hôtel de Ville. When he allowed the National Guard to fire on the riotous assembly in the Champ de Mars on July 17, 1791, he lost his popularity. Arrested on September 6, 1793, he was executed on November 12th in atonement for his «crime of July 17th».

Barère Bertrand (1755-1841)

Advocate, elected to the estates-general after the Convention, he became an important member of the Committee of Public Safety where he dealt with foreign affairs, public instruction, and military matters. Held in high esteem by Robespierre, it was not until he realized that all was lost that he sided with his adversaries. But it was too late and he was proscribed and imprisoned at the Saintes from where he escaped to live in hiding until 18 Brumaire.

Barnave Antoine (1761-1793)

Advocate, elected to the estates-general and then to the Convention, he was one of the greatest orators of the Constituent Assembly. In 1790, together with Duport and Lameth, he fought Mirabeau's policies and founded the club of the Feuillants after the incident of the Champ de Mars. But since he later defended the position of the Court and counseled a constitutional monarchy he was arrested and beheaded on November 28, 1793.

Barras Paul (1755-1829)

A member of the Convention who voted the death penalty for the king, he was sent to the south of France in 1793 where he was responsible for bloody reprisals. Recalled to Paris, he participated in the conspiracy against Robespierre, and had him arrested at the Hôtel de Ville on 9 Thermidor. He became the strong man of the Thermidorians, and with Napoleon's aid he put down the Royalist uprising of 13 Vendémiaire. Appointed to the Directory the following month, he eliminated the Royalist and Jacobin extremists and was then in turn ousted by Bonaparte after the coup d'etat of 18 Brumaire.

Beaumarchais Pierre Augustin (1732-1799)

Author of the *Barber of Seville* (1775) and the *Marriage of Figaro* (1784), Beaumarchais cheerfully mixed his talents as a dramatist with those of a negotiator and business man. Entrusted by the Revolutionary government with the recuperating of arms stored in Holland which he never delivered, he was interned in the prison of the Abbaye. Liberated only a few days before the massacres of September, he forthwith fled to London, and did not return to France until after Robespierre's death.

Billaud-Varenne Jacques Nicolas (1756-1819)

Lawyer, elected to the Convention, he voted in favor of the death of the king and played an important role in the downfall of the Girondins. An ardent Jacobin, he became a member of the Committee of Public Safety in September of 1793, upholding Robespierre's policies and pronouncing himself against Hébert and Danton. Even though he opposed the Incorruptible on 8 Thermidor, he soon irritated the Thermidorians who had him condemned and deported to French Guiana on May 20, 1795.

Bonaparte Napoleon (1769-1821)

Born in Ajaccio, Corsica, as a young officer he adhered to the Revolution and swore an oath of allegiance to the Nation. In June of 1793 Barras entrusted him with the siege of Toulon, occupied by the English. After a period of disgrace for having been too loyal to the Robespierre brothers he was called in by Barras in 1795 to put down the Royalist insurrection of 13 Vendémiaire. After this, Bonaparte's star waxed ever brighter. Under the Directory he was named general in chief for the Italian campaign, then entrusted with an expedition against the English in Egypt and his crushing victories earned him great popularity. When he returned to France in 1799, he prepared the coup d'etat of 18 Brumaire with the aid of Sieyès and Talleyrand. Named first consul, then consul for life in 1800, Napoleon was consecrated emperor by the pope on December 2, 1804.

Brissot Jacques Pierre (1754-1793)

Talented publicist, in April of 1789 he launched the Girondin organ *Le Patriote françis*, which fiercely advocated the spread of Republican principles. Elected to the Legislative Assembly and then to the Convention, he became the leader of the Girondins and used all his eloquence to have war declared. But his popularity waned when he deferred the discussion on the dethronement of the king after the latter's flight to Varennes, and he compromised himself by attacking the Jacobins in his journal. Accused of conspiring against the Republic, he was arrested and sent to the guillotine on October 31, 1793.

Brune Guillaume (1763-1815)

A friend of Danton and of Marat, he was one of the founders of the club of the Cordeliers. In 1797 he was named general of division by Napoleon with whom he had gone to Italy. After the coup d'etat of 18 Brumaire, he became one of the principal collaborators of the first consul, and then fell into disgrace in 1807.

Carnot Lazare (1753-1823)

Professional officer elected to the Legislative Assembly and then to the Convention, he was seated on the side of the Montagnards (extreme revolutionary faction). Member of the Committee of Public Safety in August 1793, he took charge of the national defense and earned his nickname of «Organizer of Victory» after the victories won by the army in year II. Opposed to Robespierre, he took an active part in his downfall of 9 Thermidor. Named Director in 1795, he was soon suspected of sympathizing with the right wing and had to go into exile after the coup d'etat of 18 Fructidor.

Chabot François (1756-1794)

Former Capuchin monk at Rodez, he was one of the first to adhere to the civil constitution of the clergy. Elected to the Legislative Assembly and then to the Convention, he violently attacked the king and the monarchy, accused La Fayette of treason and preached violence and insurrection. Compromised in the affair of the liquidation of the Compagnie des Indes, he was arrested and executed on April 4, 1794.

Chaumette Pierre (1763-1794)

Editor of the journal *Révolutions de Paris*, Chaumette was the energetic animator of the club of the Cordeliers, where he ardently defended the cause of the people. After taking an active part in the insurrection of August 10, 1792 at the Tuileries, he was named a member of the insurrectional Commune. A zealous advocate of the Terror, he opposed the Girondins and frenetically threw himself into the campaign for dechristianization at the end of 1793. But he was met with profound hostility on the part of Robespierre, accused of «annihilating any kind of morality», and taken to the guillotine on April 13, 1794.

Chénier André (1762-1794)

Author and collaborator of the *Journal de Paris*, a member of the club of the Feuillants in 1791, André Chénier was a polemicist with a mordant pen. He disapproved of excess and laid the blame on Marat, whose appeals for murder he detested, and attacked the Jacobins. Included in the list of suspects after the September massacres, he was arrested on March 7, 1794 and executed on July 25th. He died unknown and his poetical works were not published until 1819.

Choderlos de Laclos Pierre (1741-1803)

The author of *Liaisons dangereuses* (1782) was also a soldier and a behind-the-scenes actor in the Revolution. A member of the club of the Jacobins, he published the *Journal des amis de la Constitution* with funds provided by the Duc d'Orléans, whose secretary he became in 1788. Hoping to place his master on the throne, after the king's flight he dictated the so-called Champ de Mars petition to Brisson. Sent on a military mission to the Pyrenees, he was arrested together with other supporters of the Duc d'Orléans on March 31, 1793. Liberated in December of 1794, he enthusiastically welcomed Napoleon's rise to power, and was entrusted by him with the defense of Taranto, where he died on September 5, 1803.

Collot d'Herbois Jean Marie (1750-1796)

Former actor and dramatic playwright, this ardent revolutionist was a popular orator and an able propagandist. Elected to the Convention and member of the Committee of Public Safety in September 1793, he ferociously repressed the uprising of Lyon. Recalled to Paris, he participated in the conspiracy against Robespierre, whom he reproached for aspiring to a dictatorship. Condemned to deportation by the Thermidorians, he was sent to Guiana, with Billaud-Varenne, in April 1795.

Condorcet Jean Antoine, Marquis de (1743-1794)

A famous mathematician with an encyclopedic knowledge, smitten with liberal ideas, he was elected to the Legislative Assembly, where he worked on a project for the reform of public education, nondenominational and based on equal rights. Reelected to the Convention, he refused to vote for the death of the king and openly opposed the Montagne, criticizing the project of the Constitution adopted on June 24, 1793. A friend of the Girondins, he was proscribed and arrested after he had stayed in hiding for some time. Imprisoned in Bourg-la-Reine, he poisoned himself in his cell on March 28, 1794.

Corday Charlotte (1768-1793)

Daughter of a pious Royalist family, Charlotte Corday was shocked by the excesses of Marat, the «September slaughterer». The evening of July 13, 1793, she gained admittance to Marat's lodgings and stabbed him to save the world and re-establish order. Immediately arrested and transferred to the Abbey prison, she was executed on July 17th.

Couthon Georges (1755-1794)

An advocate, whose legs were paralyzed, deputy to the Legislative Assembly and then to the National Convention, he seconded Robespierre in his struggle against the Girondins. Member of the Committee of Public Safety in May 1793, he was responsible for the passage of the law of 22 Prairial which reorganized the Revolutionary Tribunal and suppressed practically all warranties for those accused. Arrested with Robespierre on 9 Thermidor, he was the first to be beheaded on July 28, 1794.

Danton Georges Jacques (1759-1794)

Former advocate of the king's council, founder of the club of the Cordeliers, Danton was a powerful and stirring orator. He defended Marat, passionately attacked La Fayette and demanded the dethronement of the king. Under threat of arrest after the incident of the Champ de Mars, he was forced to seek refuge in England. When he returned to Paris he took an active part in the downfall of the king. Elected to the Convention and member of the Committee of Public Safety he was concerned above all, together with Barrère, with foreign affairs. Eliminated from the Committee in July of 1793 and tired of the excesses of the Terror, Danton, with Camille Desmoulins, initiated a campaign for moderation. Denounced by Robespierre, he refused to escape, was arrested and then executed on April 5, 1794.

123

David Jacques Louis (1748-1825)

In 1789 David placed himself at the head of the «patriot artists» and made a sketch of the oath of the Jeu de Paume. Eager to serve the Revolution, he had himself elected to the Convention, sat on the Committee of General Security, and adhered to Robespierre's party. He was entrusted with the organization of various ceremonies such as the transferral of Voltaire's ashes to the Panthéon and the pageant for the Fête of the Supreme Being. With his masterful brush he painted the scene of Marat's death, and made numerous on-the-spot sketches of those condemned under the Terror. Interned for five months in Luxembourg after Robespierre's downfall, he made an act of submission to Napoleon and became the «Emperor's painter».

Desmoulins Camille (1760-1794)

A young attorney who wholeheartedly adopted the ideas of the Revolution, on July 12, 1789 he incited the crowds in the name of liberty in the gardens of the Palais Royal. A friend of Danton and elected to the Convention, he sat with the Montagne (Mountain party), voted for the king's death and attacked Brissot and the Girondins. Disapproving however of the excesses of the Terror, he proposed moderation in *Le Vieux Cordelier*, which he launched in December 1793. Denounced to the Jacobins, he was condemned and executed together with Danton on April 5, 1794.

Fabre d'Eglantine Philippe François Fabre, known as (1750-1794)

Itinerant player-author, he was on intimate terms with Danton, for whom, together with Camille Desmoulins, he became a principal collaborator. A fanatic Revolutionary, he was elected to the Convention, where he violently attacked the enemies of the Republic. He worked for the institution of the Revolutionary calendar, adopted by the Assembly in October of 1793. Arrested on March 18, 1794, he was beheaded together with the Dantonists.

Fouquier-Tinville Antoine Quentin (1760-1795).

Former public attorney at the fortress of Châtelet, he was named public prosecutor of the Revolutionary Tribunal by his cousin Camille Desmoulins. A loyal public official, he blindly obeyed the government and went each evening to report to the Committee of Public Safety and receive orders. He drew up the indictments of the Girondins, Marie Antoinette, Barnave, the Hébertists and the Dantonists. Even though he took no sides at the time of Robespierre's downfall, the Thermidorians had him arrested and sent to the guillotine after eight months of prison, on May 7, 1795.

Guillotin Jacques Ignace (1738-1804)

Physician elected to the estates-general, he preached the principle of the equality of penalty and in January 1790 proposed that a machine already employed in Italy be used for all executions. Perfected by the German engineer Schmitt and Doctor Louis, this machine, initially called «Louison» and later «Guillotine» was used for the first time in the Place de Grève on April 15, 1792.

Hanriot François (1759-1794)

Named commander of the National Guard in May 1793 by Robespierre, he faithfully carried out his master's will and made a decisive contribution to the downfall of the Girondins on June 2, 1793. After having tried in vain to save Robespierre and his friends on 9 Thermidor, he was arrested in the Hôtel de Ville and sent to the guillotine with them.

Hébert Jacques René (1757-1794)

A virulent journalist whose language was vigorous, colorful and at times vulgar, founder of the famous *Père Duchesne*, Hébert was elected prosecutor for the Commune after August 10, 1792. Bitter opponent of the Girondins, he urged extreme measures, encouraged the policy of dechristianization and favored the cult of the goddess Reason. Arrested on orders of Robespierre for having launched an appeal for insurrection to the Cordeliers, he was executed with some of his followers on March 24, 1794.

Hérault de Séchelles Marie-Jean (1759-1794)

At attorney general introduced in the Court, he took part in the taking of the Bastille and had himself elected to the Legislative Assembly and then to the Convention. A member of the Committee of Public Safety in May 1793, he collaborated with Saint-Just in drawing up the Constitution of year I, and replaced Danton in charge of foreign affairs on July 10, 1793. President of the Convention, he was the hero of the Fête of August 10, 1793 in the Champ de Mars. Accused by Saint-Just of entertaining relations with the Austrians, he was arrested with the Dantonists and beheaded on April 5th.

La Fayette Gilbert Motier, Marquis de (1757-1837)

A young officer who had taken part in the American war of Independence, he was elected to the estates-general, where he preached the unification of the three estates. Named commander in chief of the National Guard after the fall of the Bastille, he and the mayor Bailly received the king at the Hôtel de Ville. But the incident of the Champ de Mars alienated the trust of the patriots and he had to resign form his post early in October 1791. After the insurrection of June 20, 1792 at the Tuileries, he offered his services to the king and then surrendered to the Austrians to avoid being imprisoned.

Lamballe, Princess of (1749-1792)

Widow when she was only eighteen of the Duc de Penthièvre, supervisor of the queen's household, she was arrested after the taking of the Tuileries and massacred in the prison of La Force on September 3, 1792.

Lameth Alexandre, Comte de (1760-1829)

A cavalry officer who had taken part in the American war of Independence, he was elected by the nobility to the estates-general where he joined the Third Estate. He was a member, with Barnave and Duport, of the famous «triumvirate» which defended liberal measures and founded the club of the Feuillants after the incident of Champ de Mars. During the Terror, he was reconciled with the Court and later surrendered to the Austrians with La Fayette after the insurrection of August 10, 1792.

La Revellière-Lépeaux Louis Marie de (1753-1824)

Attorney elected to the estates-general and then to the Convention, he was proscribed with the Girondins and had to go into hiding during the Terror. Only after the fall of Robespierre did he return to his seat in the Convention. Elected Director, he and Barras promoted the coup d'etat of 18 Fructidor. Obliged to resign on June 19, 1799, he refused to make common cause with Napoleon and retired from politics.

Lavoisier Antoine (1743-1794)

Father of modern chemistry, Lavoisier was also a gifted agronomist and an adept of revolutionary ideas. But because of his activity as tax collector and for having asked that a wall be constructed around Paris to reduce customs frauds to the city, he was arrested and beheaded on May 8, 1794.

Legendre Louis (1752-1797)

Uneducated but a golden-tongued orator, he incited the mob to attack the Bastille and took part in the taking of the Tuileries on August 10, 1792. Elected to the Convention, he was denounced to the Jacobins as a moderate. Attacked by Robespierre for having defended Danton, he retracted and maintained his silence until 9 Thermidor.

Le Peletier de Saint-Fargeau Louis Michel (1760-1793)

Councilor of the Paris *parlement* and a representative of the nobility in the estates-general, he became one of the most ardent advocates of the popular cause and voted for the suppression of the privileges. Elected to the Convention, he sided with the Montagnards and voted for the death of the king. Assassinated by a former body guard of Louis, XVI, named Pâris, in a cafe in the Palais Royal, his funeral was celebrated with great pomp and his mortal remains were laid to rest in the Panthéon.

Louis XVI (1754-1793)

In 1774 at the age of twenty Louis XVI became king. He was a cultured monarch, but weak in character, indecisive and with an aversion to violent measures. Forced to summon the estates general in May of 1789, he backed down in the face of their opposition, and when he was brought back to Paris after the taking of the Bastille had to swear allegiance to the Constitution in the Champ de Mars on July 14, 1790. Accusations that he had maintained secret relations with the Austrian enemy after his flight to Varennes led to the invasion of the palace of the Tuileries on August 10, 1792. The king and his family were imprisoned in the Temple and the Convention, anxious to legitimize this insurrection, brought «Louis Capet» to trial. He was condemned to death and went to the guillotine on January 21, 1793.

Marat Jean-Paul (1743-1793)

A physician who was inflamed with revolutionary ideas, in September 1789 he published the first copy of his journal *L'Ami di Peuple*, which was an immediate success. A relentless pamphleteer, he launched appeals for violence, denounced the enemies of the Revolution and extolled increasingly radical measures. Elected to the Convention, he voted for the death of the king and played an important role in the downfall of the Girondins. Hated by the moderates, he was stabbed in his bathtub by Charlotte Corday on July 13, 1793.

Marie Antoinette (1755-1793)

Daughter of Maria Teresa of Austria, she married the future Louis XVI in 1770. Surrounded by a coterie of adventurers, she incurred the hate of the populace by her frivolity. She refused all compromise with the deputies of the Assembly, urged the king to resist, incited him to flee from Paris and provoked the intervention of foreign troops. Accused of having called in the Austrians in her aid, she was condemned and executed on October 16, 1793.

Mirabeau Honoré Gabriel, Comte de (1749-1791)

After a restless youth, Mirabeau threw himself wholeheartedly into the Revolution. Elected to the estates-general, his exceptional gifts as orator and his daring propelled him to the front lines of the defenders of the rights of the Assembly. He promoted all the early reforms and incarnated the Revolution of 1789. Later, however, when he became aware of the dangers inherent in an excessively brutal reform, he attempted to impose a constitutional monarchy and renewed contacts with the Court. Soon accused of treason, his influence and popularity waned and he died of illness on April 2, 1791.

Pétion de Villeneuve Jérôme (1756-1794)

Advocate elected to the estates-general, he sat on the extreme left with Buzot and Robespierre. Elected mayor of Paris in November 1791, he supported the days of June 20th and August 10th, 1792, and kept a hands-off policy in the September massacres. Elected to the Convention and a friend of the Girondins, his vote against the death penalty for the king and his attacks on Marat alienated the confidence of the patriots. A few days after the proscription of his Girondin friends he had to flee Paris and committed suicide on June 18, 1794.

Philippe Egalité Louis-Philippe d'Orléans, known as (1747-1793)

Cousin of the king, this affable prince who was loved by the common people was elected to the estates-general by the nobility. Strongly suspected of having fomented the taking of the Bastille and the march on Versailles, the king passed him over and sent him on mission to London. On his return to Paris in July 1790 he joined the Jacobins and incited the Republicans to launch the petition of the Champ de Mars after the flight of the king. Elected to the Convention, he sat with the Montagne, and voted for the death of the king. But when his son, future Louis Philippe, surrendered to the Austrians, he became suspect and was arrested and sent to the guillotine on November 6, 1793.

Pichegru Jean-Charles (1761-1804)

Commander in chief of the army of the north, he took possession of Holland and then returned to Paris in April 1795, where he put down the popular uprising of 12 Germinal. As a result of intrigues with the Royalists, he had to resign. Elected to the Council of Five Hundred, he became president of the Assembly, carried by the Royalist majority. Deported to Guiana after the coup d'etat of 18 Fructidor, he escaped and back in Paris took part in Cadoudal's conspiracy against Napoleon.

Robespierre Maximilien de (1758-1794)

Advocate from Arras elected to the estates-general, Robespierre was an untiring, meticulous and inflexible orator who became the guding spirit of the club of the Jacobins. A member of the insurrectional Commune and then a deputy at the Convention, he pronounced himself in favor of the king's death and carried on an implacable battle against the Girondins. Elected to the Committee of Public Safety, he eliminated his principal adversaries, the Hébertists, in March of 1794, and then the Dantonists in the following month. As sole master, the «Incorruptible» (as he was known) aspired to the dictatorship, installed the Terror and had the Convention decree the recognition of the Supreme Being and the immortality of the soul. When he attacked the «corrupt» and the «traitors» at the Convention, his adversaries indicted him on 9 Thermidor. He sought refuge in the Hôtel de Ville where he was arrested, and then executed on July 28, 1794.

Roland Manon Jeanne, known as Mme (1754-1793)

Wife of Jean-Marie Roland, minister of the interior in 1792 and 1793, she kept a salon and received most of the Girondins, including Brissot, Pétion, Buzot and sometimes Robespierre himself. Extremely hostile to the Montagnards, she was arrested in June of 1793 and interned in the prison of Sainte-Pélagie where she wrote her memoirs before being guillotined on November 8th.

Roucher Antoine (1745-1794)

A poet known for his *Mois* (1769), Roucher entered politics at the beginning of the Revolution. But he was soon overwhelmed by the rising fanaticism and, having passed to the ranks of counter-revolutionary journalism, he was arrested during the Terror. Interned in the prison of Saint-Lazare, he went to the guillotine in the same tumbril with André Chénier on July 15, 1794.

Saint-Just Louis Antoine de (1767-1794)

Full of contradictions, Saint-Just was an enigmatic personality, cold-blooded and extremely proud, who dedicated himself heart and soul to the Revolution. A member of the National Guard in 1789, he took up the cause of Robespierre and remained with him until his downfall. Elected to the Convention, he became known as one of the principle orators of the Montagne as early as Louis XVI's trial. Nevertheless, in the wake of the «Incorruptible» he helped defeat the Girondins and as member of the Committee of Public Safety he fought the Hébertists and then the Dantonists. Sent on mission to the troops on the Rhine and in the north, he re-established order by exalting courage, but was also responsible for ruthless executions. Upon his return to Paris he remained faithful to Robespierre and went to the guillotine with him on 10 Thermidor.

Sieyès Emmanuel Joseph (1748-1836)

Vicar-general of Chartres, he was deeply interested in new ideas and in January of 1789 published a brochure which made him famous: *Qu'est-ce que le Tiers état? Tout*. Elected to the estates-general he demanded the union of the three orders and drew up the text of the Tennis Court oath. But he was later eclipsed by more brilliant orators and his projects for the Constitution were indifferently received and rejected. Elected to the Convention, he sat with the Center (Marais) and abstained from all the important deliberations. Deputy to the Council of Five Hundred, then a member of the Directory in May 1795, he rallied to Napoleon's side, upon the advice of Talleyrand. Named provvisory Consul on the eve of 19 Brumaire, he was replaced a month later by Cambaceres.

Talleyrand-Périgord Charles Maurice de (1754-1838)

Bishop of Autun, he entered the order without a vocation and was elected to the estates-general by the Clergy. In October 1789 he presented a project for the nationalization of the property of the Church. As soon as the civil constitution of the clergy was adopted he agreed to consecrate the first constitutional bishops. Sent abroad on a mission, he did not return to France until after the Terror. In July 1789 Barras nominated him minister of foreign relations for the Directory. He took part in the coup d'etat of 18 Brumaire, then, one after the other, served Napoleon, Louis XVIII and Louis-Philippe.

Tallien Jean Lambert (1767-1820)

A Montagnard deputy to the Convention, he was sent on mission to Bordeaux, where he was responsible for a violent repression. Recalled to Paris, he went over to the adversaries of Robespierre, influenced by his future wife Teresa Cabarrus, and worked for his downfall.

On September 22nd, 1792, when the Convention decreed the end of the Ancien Régime, it entrusted a committee of illustrious men with the preparation of a new calendar, which was approved in its final form on November 24th. The year was divided into twelve months of three decades each, with an additional five days (six on leap years) know as sans-culottes. This calendar remained in use until it was abolished by Napoleon on September 9, 1805.

Note: With regard to the table above, since years IV (1795-1796), VIII (1799-1800) and XII (1803-1804) were leap years, the first days in the corresponding months fall on Sept. 23rd, Oct. 23rd, Nov. 22nd, Dec. 22nd, Jan. 21 and Feb. 20th.

THE FRENCH REVOLUTIONARY CALENDAR

1	**Vendémiaire**	22 September
10		
20		11 October
30		
1	**Brumaire**	22 October
10		
20		10 November
30		
1	**Frimaire**	21 November
10		
20		10 December
30		
1	**Nivôse**	21 December
10		
20		9 January
30		
1	**Pluviôse**	20 January
10		
20		8 February
30		
1	**Ventôse**	19 February
10		
20		10 March
30		
1	**Germinal**	21 March
10		
20		9 April
30		
1	**Floréal**	20 April
10		
20		9 May
30		
1	**Prairial**	20 May
10		
20		8 June
30		
1	**Messidor**	19 June
10		
20		8 July
30		
1	**Thermidor**	19 July
10		
20		7 August
30		
1	**Fructidor**	18 August
10		
20		6 September
30		
1	**Sans-culottes**	17 September
5		21 September

CONTENTS

Introduction .... page 2

The Revolution in the history of Paris .... " 3
- The Fall of the Bastille ...... " 3
- The Constituent Assembly ... " 9
- The Legislative Assembly .... " 11
- The Convention .... " 16
- The Directory .... " 24

Le Marais, les Halles les Iles .... " 26
- The Bastille .... " 26
- Temple de la Visitation Sainte-Marie .... " 32
- Arcade de Bretonvilliers ...... " 32
- The Theater of Beaumarchais " 32
- La Force .... " 33
- House 113 bd. Beaumarchais " 35
- Ancien Théâtre 117 rue Vieille du Temple .... " 35
- The Temple .... " 36
- Les Madelonnettes .... " 39
- Conservatoire des Arts et Métiers .... " 40
- Intersection rue de Cléry-boulevard Saint-Denis ...... " 40
- Place du Caire .... " 40
- Church of Saint-Eustache .... " 41
- The Cour Batave .... " 41
- Place de Grève .... " 42
- Tour Saint-Jacques .... " 47
- Palais de Justice .... " 48
- Conciergerie .... " 50
- Pont-Neuf .... " 54

The Louvre, the Quarter of the Palais Royal, the Grands Boulevards .... " 58
- The Louvre .... " 58
- Place du Carrousel .... " 63
- Palais des Tuileries and Gardens .... " 64
- Palais Royal .... " 72
- Le Boeuf à la mode .... " 75

- The Church of Saint-Roch .. " 75
- The Jacobins .... " 76
- The Guillotine and its first itinerary .... " 78
- Robespierre's Lodgings ...... " 79
- Place Vendôme .... " 80
- Hôtel 1-3 rue d'Antin .... " 80
- Rue des Colonnes .... " 81
- Musée Grévin .... " 81
- Hôtel d'Augny .... " 81
- Hôtel Botterel-Quintin .... " 81
- Hôtel Bourrienne .... " 81
- The Saint-Lazare Prison ..... " 82
- Hôtel Pinsot .... " 82
- Rue de la Victoire .... " 82
- Hôtel Lakanal .... " 82
- The Chapelle Expiatoire ..... " 84
- Place de la Révolution .... " 85

The Faubourg Saint-Germain .... " 91
- Champ de Mars .... " 91
- Auberge du Soleil d'Or ...... " 92
- Hôtel 83 rue du Cherche-Midi " 93
- Hôpital Laënnec .... " 93
- Old Convent of the Recollets " 93
- Hôtel de Galliffet .... " 93
- Hôtel de Chanaleilles .... " 93
- Hôtel de Castries .... " 94
- Hôtel de Villars .... " 94
- Hôtel Chanac de Pompadour " 95
- Palais Bourbon .... " 95
- Hôtel de Seignelay .... " 95
- Hôtel de Salm .... " 95
- Hôtel de Roquelaure .... " 96
- Old entrance to the Convent of the Theatines .... " 96
- The Musée des Monuments Français .... " 96
- Maison de Buzot .... " 97
- Hôtel de Chateauneuf .... " 98
- Chapelle de la Charité .... " 98
- St.-Germain-des-Prés .... " 98
- House 6 rue Grégoire de Tours .... " 100

- Café Procope .... " 100
- Hôtel 16 rue de l'Ancienne Comédie .... " 100
- Cour du Commerce .... " 101
- House 10 rue de la Huchette " 101

The Latin Quarter .... " 102
- Place Henri Mondor .... " 102
- Faculté de Médecine .... " 103
- The Cordeliers .... " 104
- House of Desmoulins .... " 105
- House 15 rue Servandoni .... " 105
- Church of Saint-Sulpice ...... " 106
- Les Carmes .... " 107
- Rue Madame et rue de Fleurus " 109
- Palais du Luxembourg .... " 110
- The Communs of Luxembourg " 111
- The Luxembourg Gardens ... " 111
- The Pantheon .... " 112
- Café 2 rue des Fossés Saint-Jacques .... " 113
- Café 40 rue de la Montagne Sainte-Geneviève .... " 114
- Saint-Nicolas du Chardonnet " 114
- Collège des Bernardins .... " 114
- Collège des Ecossais .... " 114
- Port-Royal .... " 115
- House 23 rue Jean Dolent ... " 115
- The Salpêtrière .... " 116

Jardin des Plantes La Nation .... " 117
- The Guillotine and its last itinerary .... " 117
- Church of Sainte-Marguerite " 118
- The Revolt of the Manufacture Reveillon .... " 118
- Place du Trône Renversé ..... " 119
- Picpus .... " 120
- The Belhomme Boarding House .... " 122

The Leading Figures of the Revolution .... " 123

The French Revolutionary Calendar .... " 125

CREDITS:

Photos from the Archives of Casa Editrice Bonechi taken by Pinheira:
1; 28a; 31a, b; 32; 35a, b; 39a, b; 40; 43; 47; 50; 51b; 54a; 63; 64a; 73b; 75a; 76a; 79; 80a, b; 81a, b; 84a, b; 87a; 90b; 92b; 93a, b; 95; 96a, b; 98a, b; 100a, b; 101a, b; 102; 103a, b; 104a, b; 105a, b; 106a; 107a, b; 108; 109; 110; 112a; 113b; 114; 115a, b; 116; 117; 118a, b; 119; 120; 121a, b; 122.

© Photos Musées Nationaux:
55; 59; 60-61; 83; 97a.

© Photos B.N. Cabinet des Estampes:
8b; 12a; 22b; 33; 34; 38a; 41; 73a; 78; 94; 106b.

© Photos Caisse Nationale des Monuments Historiques CNMHS / SPADEM: 52a, b.

Photos Musées de la Ville de Paris © by SPADEM 1987:
6; 8a; 9; 10b; 11; 12b; 13; 14; 14-15; 16; 18a; 19; 22a; 23; 24a, b; 30a; 36; 37; 38b; 44-45; 46a; 48; 49; 51a; 53; 54b; 56-57; 62-63; 64b; 68a, b; 69; 72; 74; 75b; 76b; 77; 85; 86a, b; 87b; 91; 97b; 99; 111; 112b.

G. Dagli Orti:
3; 4-5; 6-7; 10a; 18b; 20; 21; 25; 26-27; 28-29; 30b; 42; 46b; 58; 65; 66-67; 70-71; 88-89; 90a; 92a.